FROM THE LOVE OF WISDOM . . .

A NEW VIEW OF BEING HUMAN

The Pioneers of Kinlein

This edition published by
Dog Ear Publishing
4010 W. 86th Street, Ste H
Indianapolis, IN 46268

www.dogearpublishing.net

ISBN: 978-145750-706-9
This book is printed on acid-free paper.

Printed in the United States of America

CONTRIBUTORS

Grace K. F. Bates, CPK
Mary L. Bolin, CPK
Ann Cameron, CPK
Karen Carpenter, CPK
Claudia Fujinaga, CPK
Mary Ann Glynn, CPK
Sally Greene, CPK
Annette James, CPK
Nancy Kohorn Henricks, CPK
Jeanette Tedesco, CPK
M. Joanne Torrey, CPK
Loretta Ulmschneider, CPK
Linda Waggoner, CPK

EDITORS

Grace K. F. Bates, CPK
Mary L. Bolin, CPK
Loretta Ulmschneider, CPK

This book is the first to be written by the first learners of the Theory of Moving in Esca. These kinleiners are called pioneers because they glimpsed the goodness and potential benefit for all people, left familiar territory in other fields, and helped forge the frontiers of a new profession. The book began as an assignment to a class of certified kinleiners who were preparing themselves to teach the theory of moving in esca. The year was 1998. The assignment was to select a concept within the theory of moving in esca and write a chapter for a book. The original material, used as a source for all of the concepts, sub-concepts and processes, was developed by M. Lucille Kinlein, author of the theory and Founder of the Profession of Kinlein. Kinleiners took the assignment seriously and selected editors in 1999 to review the chapters and coordinate the material for eventual publication. Each of the kinleiners named above wrote something for that assignment; something that has been carried forward into this book. Without the contributions of each person, the book could not have been written.

The Editors

TABLE OF CONTENTS

ACKNOWLEDGEMENTS

No book ever is published without the efforts of others in addition to the writers. The editors and authors of this book wish to acknowledge with gratitude, those contributions. Some of those identified may not have written a word but their work was important in bringing the book from an idea to a finished project.

Thank you, Katie Alley for the graphic designs that grace our pages. Your diagrams provide a visual and concrete dimension to the very abstract ideas presented in words.

Thank you to the American Kinlein Association, which funded the publication of this book and to its Kinleiner of Reference, Nancy Kohorn Henricks, CPK who knew that it would be helpful to all who read it

Thank you Rita Martin, MK, CPK, for your copyediting, proof reading and other helpful suggestions. The book is stronger and more finished because of your work.

Thank you Linda Waggoner, MS, CPK who gathered up all the details of publication (and there were many), encouraged and cajoled us to make decisions, and who fulfilled the responsibility of getting the pages from pages to BOOK. Without her efforts, the manuscript might still be just that.

Finally, thank you to M. Lucille Kinlein, MSN (Ed), CPK, the first Kinleiner. She followed her call to help people; she developed the concepts described in this book; and she continues to teach us and guide us.

The Editors

INTRODUCTION

The purpose of this book is to introduce to the world a new view of being human. This view is based on the premises that (1) at conception a person receives the power to take action in living life on a day to day basis, the power to move through life; (2) a person knows him- or herself better than anyone else can know him or her; (3) dignity is a quality of being human. This view contains profound implications for the way we humans interact with one another and for the way that we conduct ourselves in all aspects of living our lives. If I have "the power to take action in living life on a day to day basis", then I am in control of the actions I take and I am responsible for the results. If I know myself better than anyone else knows me, then what I say about myself has significance and I will want to listen carefully to what others say about themselves for their words also are significant. If dignity is a quality of being human then I will respond to all persons with respect. If I conduct myself from this perspective and interact with others from this perspective, a whole new light is shed on human beings in relationship. I am FREE from prejudicial or categorical restraints to be true to myself, and to hold regard for others.

The theory which underlies this view of being human, identifies and names the intangible processes within a person which precede any action taken, any word spoken, any feeling experienced. From the "movings" in these processes, and the resulting actions, the uniqueness of any one human being emerges amidst the universal qualities that comprise all human beings. It is this uniqueness that makes me, me, and you, you.

This view of the human being was first identified and described by M. Lucille Kinlein, educator, theorist, author, and founder of the Profession of Kinlein. She thought the view she had of people was commonly held, but as she observed and participated in a variety of personal and professional interactions, she found her perspective to be fairly unique. Coming from a field that took *care of*, provided *care for*, and gave *care to* others, which effectively made the person a passive receiver of care, Kinlein opened a practice of *caring with* people. She listened to them and recognized the gold in their words. From that practice, came a theory called the Theory of Moving in Esca, or the Theory of That Moving Power in Every Human Being to Take Action in Living Life on a Day-to-Day Basis. From the development of the theory, a profession was born. Through the profession and its educational and research activities, kinleiners are now assisting people as they live through the things life brings.

This book describes concepts and processes in human beings that previously have been unnamed. Thirteen different authors tackled the description of the different aspects of the theory and three editors brought the writings into a whole. The character and uniqueness of each chapter with its own author allows the chapters to stand alone, yet each chapter lends a flow with the chapter preceding and the chapter following providing cohesion to the reading.

The focus of this theory, the power of the human being to take action, provides the perspective that every person makes a difference as life is lived. That difference is based upon the answers each one forms to the humble and profound questions of the common man: Who am I? Why am I here? What am I doing with who I am?

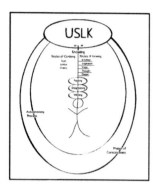

CHAPTER 1   A NEW LIGHT ON AN OLD QUESTION

This book begins with a mystery. Since a mystery is defined as something that cannot be fully explained or understood, this book will also end with a mystery. What makes up a human being? What is the true nature of being human? It is hoped that the pages between beginning and end will intrigue and inspire the reader and shed some new light on these old questions.

The challenge of understanding the complexity of human beings has sparked the development of many fields of study that delve into certain aspects or parts of human nature. Physiologists describe details of the amazing workings of the human body. Psychology provides theories about human behavior, motivation and the development of the intellect. Theology addresses matters of the spirit or soul and the question of the ultimate "Why?" of everything. Each of these disciplines investigates a *singular* aspect of human beings as a separate entity: body, mind (psyche), or spirit (soul). From the singular focus on a part given by these disciplines, inferences are made as to the nature of the whole human being. When parts are the starting point, the questions that follow relate to how the parts are connected to each other. Inevitably the answers to such questions fall short of providing a true picture of the whole human being. Something is missing

1

because the whole is greater than the sum of the parts.

Questions relating to the nature and essence of something belong to the first science, philosophy. It uses the tool of reason to explore all things knowable to our unaided powers, when these things are studied in their deepest, ultimate causes and reasons. In so doing, philosophy looks at the essence of things. Because of the magnitude of its scope, the science of philosophy holds promise for providing answers to the questions posed.

A philosophical theory developed by M. Lucille Kinlein sheds a new light on the nature of human beings. Unlike philosophers whose quests were focused only in the intellectual realm, Kinlein's path took a different route. Academic degrees in languages, nursing and nursing education gave her a firm foundation in many subjects, including philosophy; however, the theory she developed was not an armchair endeavor. It began within the vision of Kinlein, a nurse who wanted to offer her caring to people without the constraints that the medical care system imposed. She saw that there was a kind of "gold" inside people that got them through the long days and hard nights. Medicine helped to patch people back together in a time of crisis, and then they went home to deal with the rest of their lives. *Kinlein wanted to help people build on what was already inside them.* She knew that the way to do that involved the simple, profound, and caring act of listening. When people sought help from doctors, lawyers and the clergy, she observed, "There was no opportunity for them to speak where they were, without having the listener put what was said into a box that referred to the listener's field . . . So I thought it was time for the person to be listened to from any point of departure that the client wanted to depart from."[1] In 1971 she followed her intuition that said now was the time to act on her vision. Kinlein opened a practice in an office setting as an independent generalist nurse, the first nurse in the world to establish a practice independent of the practice of medicine.[2]

The clients came, one by one. Kinlein would begin appointments by saying, "Wherever you would like to start..." As the clients spoke about themselves, she realized something was coming into focus for her regarding caring and regarding the uniqueness of each person.

Kinlein says, "Now I know I was seeing a phenomenon at work in the clients... I was trying to make the (nursing) concept fit and it wouldn't, so I turned away from that concept and focused on the phenomenon - whatever it was - that I was *seeing in the clients' words.* It was there in the words and I had to work to grasp it...." [3] As she shifted her focus to this phenomenon in the human being, Kinlein described a sense of awe and wonder that must be similar to that which a laboratory scientist feels when some unexpected particle is seen for the first time. Perhaps it is also comparable to the joy felt in every philosopher's heart when the truth of an essence is revealed and all that obscured it falls away.

The phenomenon observed by Kinlein was named <u>e</u>xercise of <u>s</u>elf <u>c</u>are <u>a</u>gency. Later the acronym, **esca,** was adopted and defined as **that moving power in every human being to take action in living life on a day-to-day basis.** Later still a profound coincidence was discovered. *Esca* is also a Latin word defined as food or sustenance for a journey, in this case, the journey of life.

The "gold" inside the person that Kinlein had seen dimly from the beginning gained luster and clarity as it was named and studied as seen in the clients' words. The light of Lucille Kinlein's desire to care with people in a different way illuminated a phenomenon that had never before been given such attention. In no other field had there been "a singular focus on the nature of that power a person has to move himself or herself through life."[4]

In the late 70's there was this quote from a client: "I tell my neighbor I am going for kinleining with my kinleiner." It became clear to Kinlein that what she was identifying was much broader than nursing. It was a universal phenomenon of the human being. The focus and formal object of her practice was not disease, but rather the person moving in esca. As the practice grew, others requested classes to learn what Kinlein was doing and how she was doing it. It became evident to her that she was no longer practicing nursing, but was practicing something new. Therefore, in August of 1979, the profession of kinlein was founded.

As the profession grew, two theories were articulated. The first one came from the words clients spoke in appointments, which provided evidence of the phenomenon of moving in esca. This "gold" inside every person is described by the theory of moving in esca and is the subject of this book. The second theory addresses the practice of kinlein: how a kinleiner assists persons in moving in esca. Although the assisting theory is referenced at times, it is not the focus of this book.

Human beings have always known that they have the power to take action in life. They have thought, decided, invented, walked, sung, digested, breathed, pondered, prayed, wondered, feared, enjoyed, grieved and taken many other actions of intellectual, physiological, spiritual and excitational natures. <u>What is new is to look at these actions as integrated aspects of that moving power within each person.</u> This way of viewing the human being provides a contrast to the one produced by examining the separate pieces of mind, body, spirit and emotions. Residing in the field of philosophy, this theory builds on facts garnered from the other sciences to present a new view of the human being.

This book speaks to "a power that is able to be proven through philosophical argument to exist at the moment of the *Being* of life, which is at the moment of the union of the ovum and the sperm which creates a third person.... The exercise of that power is called moving in esca and it begins at the moment that the cells begin to mitose in the formation of the corporeal self of a human being...." [5] Since there is no evidence to support that the exercise of this moving power begins at a later point in time, it is logical to assume that it begins when a human life begins.

"The power is **universal**. It exists in every human being who is living. It existed in every human being who has ever lived. It will exist in every human being who will ever live. It is **intrinsic** in

4

every human being. The nature of the power and the exercise of it is the same in every human being; but the form and characteristics of it are **unique** to every human being and **are as uniquely one's own as are one's fingerprints......**" This is one of the paradoxes of human beings: so much is held in common by all, yet each one is different.   Even the metabolism within the body has been documented by science as being unique in each person. "It would be a totally different world were we all the same in any one aspect."[6]

This moving power to take action in living life is **ineluctable.** It can never not be exercised. Persons are moving in esca when they are two seconds, two days or two decades old, up until the moment of their deaths. Persons are moving in esca when they are asleep, in a coma, drunk, brain dead, experiencing sensory deprivation or physical limitations, acting morally or immorally, facing challenges or succumbing to despair, feeling grief, anger or joy, sustaining health or living with illness. "The notion of the **ongoingness......**of the exercising, of the moving, of that power must remain in focus constantly, because that is the reason that one can *change* at any given moment, and act in light of a different frame of reference or motive...If the image of a circle can be applied to the continuum of the nature of life, then one can choose any point of the circle as the best time to initiate change, because there is no one best point on a circle at which change should be started. There is always a time when some action can be initiated by a person...

Moving in esca is <u>good in and of itself</u>. The consequences of actions taken in moving in esca may not be good in the sense that the person regrets having thought, said, felt, decided or done something.   In addition, the result of any action may bring harm to the Self of the person or to other persons, but that does not make the power not good.   The frame of reference, the motives may not be good, but the power to act that way is good and is <u>inviolable</u> by another person."[7]

The consequences of the choices made are the responsibility of the person who made them. "Hence, the privilege of moving in esca has implicit in it a twofold responsibility, namely to self, for the way one lives one's life, and, at the same time, to others who also have the same power with the same responsibility...**There is no point in life at which the person does not have control over his/her actions. There is no point in life at which the person does not have responsibility for his/her actions. Ultimately a choice was made at some point in time for which the person now bears accountability."**[8]

With this awesome responsibility comes a great freedom. "One determines one's own destiny and how to accomplish the achievement of that destiny through... that [moving] power within..."[9] Is it true that humans have this much freedom in <u>any</u> circumstance? Here, it must be recognized that freedom is distinct from liberty. Liberties can be taken away by changes in a government or by force. Though people may have little or no control over situations in which they find themselves, they still retain what Viktor Frankl called "the last inner freedom." Speaking of his experience as a prisoner in Nazi concentration camps, Frankl concludes: "Fundamentally therefore any man can, even under such circumstances, decide what shall become of him - mentally and spiritually." [10] Human freedom lies, then, within the person, within that moving power to take action in living life. No one can take this power away from a person.

No one else can measure it. Since it is unique in every human being, "It is impossible for another human being to know the degree of the power or the ways in which the power will be energized and manifested."[11] In the theory of moving in esca, the potential of a human being is not seen as fixed, but rather as having the capability to expand with geometric progression. "Maturity discloses unfulfilled potential, so the more mature a person becomes, the more a person actualizes his talents, skills, uniqueness, the more that person discovers that it's possible to think, feel, do, or accomplish... People speak of someone fulfilling his potential as though there were a mark of fulfillment of potential. Because of the geometric progression idea, one <u>level</u> of potential is fulfilled and it opens up a level twice as encompassing, so it's ever expanding and never fulfilled."[12]

    Esca, that moving power in every human being to take action in living life is
> a **given** from the moment of conception,
>> **ongoing,** until the last breath,
>>> **ineluctable,**
>>> **a paradox:**
>>>> **universal** to all persons, yet
>>>> **unique** in each one;
>>>>> **good in and of itself,**
>>>>>> a **responsibility,**
>>>>>>> **inviolable,**
>>>>>> able to **expand potential**.

    Looking at all of these features of that moving power allows one to see human beings and self in a new light. This perspective highlights the **innate dignity of every person**. Dignity comes from the Latin, *dignitas,* defined as worthy. All people are worthy of esteem and respect because they have been given the gift of life and the gift of moving in esca. Neither illness, pain, occupation nor economic status can diminish this innate dignity. This theory does not attempt to group or categorize people by characteristics or behaviors they hold in common. It does identify universal qualities and processes present in every human being and emphasizes the uniqueness of each person.

    This book provides the reader with an introduction to a theory about the dynamics of being human. This theory begins to answer the questions, "What makes up a human being? What is the true nature of being human?" It is called the theory of moving in esca or, the theory of that moving power in every human being to take action in living life on a day-to-day basis. In a world where the nature of reality is often narrowed to only that which can be perceived by the senses or measured with a machine, a new light on what it means to be a human being has never been more needed. Ideas about what is real, important and necessary form the foundation of the lives of individuals and societies. The closer an idea or system of knowledge matches objective reality, the more reliably it will help individuals in navigating life and developing harmonious relationships with others. The simplest of truths, when observed in our daily lives, has an amazing power to reveal a path through the maze. What we focus on does grow. When categories, labels and diagnoses become the primary lens for viewing ourselves and others, our vision becomes distorted and fragmented. When the inviolable power we each have to act and the uniqueness of each person taking action becomes our primary lens, the light of truth and beauty in self and others can be more clearly seen.

---

[1] Kinlein, M.Lucille, unpublished interview with Annette. James. August 24, 2004

[2] Kinlein, M. Lucille, Independent Nursing Practice with Clients (Philadelphia: Lippincott Company, 1977) (for additional information)

[3] James, Annette. "Interview with M. Lucille Kinlein," Journal of Esca, Oct. 1996., p. 8

[4] Kinlein, M.Lucille, Moving That Power Within, 1985. (Minneapolis, Minnesota: National Center of Kinlein, 1985), p. xiv.

[5] Kinlein, M. Lucille, op.cit., p. 38

[6] Kinlein, M.Lucille., op cit, p. xiv

[7] Kinlein, M.Lucille, op. cit,, pp. 44-45

[8] Kinlein, M.Lucille, op cit p. xiv, pp. 44-45

[9] Kinlein, M.Lucille, op cit, p. xiv

[10] Frankl, Viktor, Man's Search for Meaning, (New York: Washington Square Press, 1964) p. 105

[11] Kinlein, M.Lucille, op cit, p. 45

[12] James, Annette, op. cit, p. 8

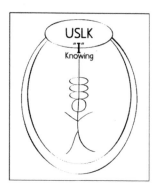

CHAPTER 2   "I" AND "MY SELF"

"No system can be understood completely from the properties of its constituent parts. On the contrary, the properties of the parts can only be understood from the dynamics of the whole. Ultimately there are no parts at all, only patterns in an inseparable web of relationship." [1]

A newborn child has 50 trillion cells at birth and in each second of our lives there are six trillion reactions taking place in each of our cells.[2] Can you imagine it?

What governs all this activity? What keeps order and balance? Some people think it is the brain; yet physiologists have discovered that the chemical messengers once thought to be made and sent only by the brain are in fact, made and sent by many other cells in the body. How do those cells "know" how to do that? They are all pieces of a whole, but what holds that whole together?

Right now, as you read these words, what is making your thoughts and responses? Is it possible for something concrete and physical to be the **source** of something as ephemeral as a thought?

What is it in a human being that contemplates life's experiences, summons courage, and experiences love? What wills and intends and controls one's actions? What knows the purpose and meaning of one's own life? What knows and observes values?

What produces the feelings of joy, despair, anger, grief, anticipation? What sustains them? What stops them?

Ninety-eight percent of the atoms in a human body are replaced each year. What holds the memories and the essence of a person, if the body's structural elements are changed so often? [2]

The answer to all these questions is one word, comprised of one letter: "I".

In the theory of moving in esca it is **the metaphysical "I" of the person that is the ultimate source of control of "my Self". "The "I" of a person cannot be divided into parts; it is whole, entire and absolutely indivisible.** It is greater than the sum of the parts of Self..." [3]

Since *metaphysics*, which is a branch of philosophy, examines the nature of reality and the relationship between mind and matter, it is important to ask how this "I" relates to mind and to matter. The theory of moving in esca states that the "I" was conceived in a state of knowing, called **"I" Knowing**. "All else flows from this knowing." [4] This metaphysical "I" is in every cell of the person and is called **"I" Cellular**. In the theory of moving in esca, **it is the "I" of the person that unifies "mind" and "body".**

"I" Knowing

"I" Knowing is the state of a human being from the moment of conception onward throughout life to death. This concept refers to the intrinsic quality of the discernment of these three realities:
- the universal source of life and knowledge
- right and wrong, good and evil

- life and death.
In its essence, the "I" Knowing is universal, but each person responds uniquely to this knowing and in this knowing throughout life [5].

"I" Knowing also contains:
- knowing something about the purpose and meaning of "my" life
- knowing that I know
- limits of my knowing. I know that I don't know everything.

In considering the concept of "I" Knowing, it might be helpful to look at some philosophical arguments for and against the idea that a human being is conceived in a state of knowing. To argue that human beings were conceived with<u>out</u> knowing, one would have to account for how children know that certain actions are wrong, even though their parents or other adults have said or done otherwise. If humans were conceived with a blank slate, not knowing anything until they were taught it, wouldn't it be much easier for parents and others to fill a child with fantasies and dreams of who they should become? Many common human experiences lend validity to the concept of "I" Knowing. Anyone who can remember the sting of an injustice or the certainty that characterizes a moment of finding truth, can touch the solidity of such knowing in self. Was there not a knowing, an inner map that the reader consulted at each major turning point in life? Though this knowing was intangible and perhaps wordless, wasn't it so real that you felt uneasy or became sick, if you did not act in accord with it? When you followed this inner knowing didn't a "yes" reverberate throughout your being?

"I" Knowing begins at the beginning of each human life. Each person can gain greater understanding of this knowing as life unfolds.

"I" Cellular

Let's take a closer look at the concept of "I" Cellular by

11

asking, Where is this metaphysical "I" of the person that was conceived in a state of knowing? Because it is metaphysical it is not confined or limited to one place. The "I" of the person exists in the cells of the body, in the electromagnetic aura surrounding the body, and outside of the body. Since every human being began as one cell, this metaphysical "I" was present in that one cell and continued to be present as that first cell divided and grew into 2, 4, 16, 256. . . .to 50 trillion cells. *"I" Cellular is "I" in myself in every cell of my body.* [6] "I" exist in a causal, material world; therefore, the cells that "I" exist in receive the results of moving in esca. "I" will, intend, pay attention, organize, find meaning, observe values, remember, wonder, love, think, judge, enjoy, desire, grive; and every cell of my body responds to these actions. As "I" breathe, work, wonder, study and feel, "I" come to understand what "I" know. **All knowing must pro-cess through the cells of the body for consummation of understanding in living, because "I" in myself is in every cell of my body."** [7]

As one ponders the quality or state of being "I", one arrives at **"I"-ness,** the essence of human life. "I am, therefore I breathe, I am in the state of knowing that I am. It is the complexity of the human being in his elemental component, the *sine qua non* of the person." [8]

"I" exist.

"I" exist in a state of knowing: <u>"I" Knowing</u>.

"I" exist in every cell of "my" body: <u>"I" Cellular.</u>

There is only one "I", whole and indivisible, conceived in a state of knowing, present in every cell, controlling "my Self."

"My Self"

If this is true then, that the "I" of the person cannot be reduced or divided into parts, how can we talk about the parts of the Self? Is *Self* different from *I* ? Are they not words that refer to the same reality, the same being? In the dictionary, *self* is defined as one's total being. *I* is defined as a pronoun used to refer to one's self. The difference therefore between *I* and *self* is the <u>relationship</u> of the speaker to the word. These two words denote different views of the <u>same</u> reality. It is the change in view from subjective to objective. For example, when I use "I" to refer to myself, I am on the inside unified and whole, looking out. When I look at "my Self", I must take a step back. "My Self" then comes into view as an object. Although this "Self" is whole and unified, I can see different aspects, or parts of "my Self".

The "parts" of a human being make sense only in the context of the whole. Although some people see these "parts" as separate entities, having meaning outside of the whole, Kinlein states unequivocally, "No part of a human being is ever separated from another part. The "I" controlling Self Animate and Self Corporeal is all one." [9]

Physicists attempt to explain the nature and workings of the physical world. How much more complex it is to explain something about the nature and workings of human beings. Though one can be certain that "I" exist, how can anyone fully explain what changed from the moment the last breath was breathed until the moment after breath ceases. This is the mystery of Life. "I" exist. "I" control "my Self". "My Self" has an aspect that is invisible, intangible, and inaudible: **Self Animate.** "My Self" has an aspect that is visible, tangible, audible: **Self Corporeal**. These two aspects are so united as a human being lives life that they cannot be separated and are termed , **Self Animate-Corporeal** in this theory. By highlighting the unique features of each aspect, greater understanding can be gained of the whole human being.

Self*Animate*-Corporeal

Self animate is the invisible, intangible, inaudible aspect of a person. It is that which animates, gives life to, moves, the cells of the body. It is part of the mystery of what is no longer present after a person breathes the last breath. The concept of self animate encompasses actions that have been referred to as belonging to the "mind" or the "spirit" of a human being. Examples of such actions

include: willing,   loving,   knowing,   thinking,   dreaming,
remembering, and "seeing" something more clearly.

Can any one of these actions be explained satisfactorily as the
results of the working of the cells of the brain and the rest of the
body? If humans are simply biological machines, what's running
that machine? Can a machine - even the most advanced computer
- question why it exists? Can it question it's own programming?
If humans are only material and physical in nature, how can such a
nature produce something as immaterial, yet real as:
                love,
                        courage,
                                faith
                                        or a thought?

The brain does not produce a thought. It is the receptor of
thought.   The heart does not produce love.   Its cells are the
receptors of love. Though the heart has long been identified with
love and the brain with thought, every cell in the human body is
affected by thought, by love, by joy or sorrow. [10]

The wholeness of Self does not imply an undifferentiated blob.
To understand human nature, it is important to grasp the union of
two different natures - animate and corporeal, intangible and
tangible - united in one being. The intricate complexity of the
human body provides living structures whose patterns are poised to
respond to the complex, ephemeral movings in self animate.
Though invisible, these movings are real. They are more powerful
than the visible body because movings in self animate are the
source of every word spoken, every action taken by a human
being. Self Animate is like the piano player. The piano, beautiful
as it may be, cannot produce music without someone to move the
keys. The music played contains the order necessary to express the
purpose and intent of the composer and the musician. "I", moving
in that moving power within, use "my Self" for a purpose. It is the
animate nature of that Self that designs and produces an order to
carry out some purpose.

"I" must engage in many discreet and complex processes in self animate to accomplish any purpose. Though invisible, self animate has both order and structure. "I" cannot accomplish any purpose without suitable means and tools. In each action "I" takes, the will, intellect and emotions are all involved. Each big "chunk action" that "I" takes is composed of many little actions. For example, baking a pie might involve finding, measuring, sifting, blending, and pouring various ingredients. None of these overt, visible actions could have occurred without the "I" of the person engaging in many intangible actions such as: willing, intending, paying attention, and organizing. All of these words ending in *ing* connote a process. **A *process* is defined as *a systematic series of actions directed to some end.*** The processes of measuring and blending have different purposes, requiring distinct means; so, too, the unseen actions of "I", moving in that moving power within, have different purposes requiring distinct means.

Visible overt actions involve processes that are undertaken in a linear sequence: first, measure; then, sift; next, stir, and so on; whereas, the invisible actions of self animate involve the "I" engaging in many processes simultaneously. For example, at the same time as a person is measuring, sifting and stirring, the "I" of that person also is paying attention, registering sensations, coordinating muscular activity and more. The complexity of what goes on in a human being in one second of time can never be fully worded or described, because of this feature of simultaneity.

Since Self is both Animate and Corporeal at once, the "I" receives the results of all these many processes of self animate in every cell of "my" body. In light of this phenomenon, the next question becomes, what is the nature of this corporeal aspect of Self?

Self Animate-*Corporeal*

The body we live in houses our self corporeal. It is the touchable, tangible, measurable, visible, aspect of self animate-

15

corporeal. Body is defined as the organized physical substance of an animal or plant, living or dead.

The surface of our corporeal self is what is seen by others. We clean and comb and put clothes on that surface. The surface can be cut open to expose blood vessels, muscles, bones, organs and connective tissue. The cells that make up the tissues can be viewed under magnification to see their parts and watch their functions. The tiniest parts of the cells can also be viewed and separated into smaller parts until the molecules are identified. All of this is self corporeal, but self corporeal is more than all of this.

In the theory of moving in esca, what completes the self corporeal is the response in every cell of the body to results of the movings in self animate. There is not an action taken, a word spoken, or a feeling experienced by a human being that is not preceded by "I" moving in self animate. Actions such as heartbeat and breathing are the manifestation in self corporeal of "I" moving in self animate; other actions include the complex chemical interactions which allow us to see, feel, digest our food, and speak, walk, and work. Self corporeal is the vehicle which the "I" uses to move through time and space. Self corporeal is more than the singular aspect of body. Self corporeal is the living human being in physical form, bearing in every cell, the intangible, non-physical "I".

The "I" has to work with matters of a spiritual nature and matters of a material nature. Receptors and transmitters in the tangible body account for evident, obvious reactions for which there is no evident, obvious stimulus. Something nonmaterial is communicated to the material body and received in every cell. The process of the cells responding to the immediate and direct effect of all the movings in the processes in self animate is termed **physiologizing**. How this happens is the mystery of the self animate "I" which cannot be touched or put into words but is present in every cell of the body.

Physiologizing is the *process* whereby the movings in self

animate affect the cells of the nervous system, the respiratory system, the musculoskeletal system, the circulatory system, the digestive system, and every other system in the physical body. The intricate process of physiologizing utilizes all parts of human physiology and results in any action of the physical body. It is generated in self animate, controlled by the "I" and manifested in self corporeal.

Physiologizing, which makes concrete the connection between self animate and self corporeal, underscores the locus of control and hence, responsibility, as being within the person. This view is in opposition to a view which puts responsibility for one's actions on one's environment, upbringing, or state of physical ability. As one comes to see oneself as responsible and with control and with choice in any situation, a sense of freedom and accountability and potency comes forth. Such is the state of human kind by nature and by design. A concept of this magnitude portends hope for the possibility that goodness can prevail in our world.

---

[1] Capra, Fritjof, "Emerging Paradigms", Poster. The Web of Life: A Scientific Understanding of Living Systems (Anchor Books, Doubleday, New York, 1996).

[2] Calhoun, Judy, Nuggets," Journal of Esca/Kinlein (June 1998, Vol.6, No. 2): p.11

[3] Kinlein, M. Lucille, op. cit., p. 57

[4] Kinlein, M. Lucille, What Am I Doing With Who I Am?, (Minneapolis: National Center of Kinlein, 1995), p. 53.

[5] Kinlein, M. Lucille; Rosin, Evelyn and Smith, Dorothy J., eds., Taxonomy for the Profession of Esca/ Practice of Kinlein, (Minneapolis: National Center of Kinlein, 1990), p. 13

[6] Kinlein, M. Lucille; Rosin, Evelyn and Smith, Dorothy J., eds., ibid., p. 13.

[7] Kinlein, M. Lucille, Moving That Power Within (Minneapolis: National Center of Kinlein, 1985) p. 65

[8] Kinlein, M. Lucille; James, Annette and Martin, Rita, The Joy of Listening (Minneapolis: National Center of Kinlein, 1993) pp. 30-31

[9] Kinlein, M. Lucille, Moving That Power Within (Minneapolis: National Center of Kinlein, 1985), p. 57.

[10] Deepak, Chopra, Quantum Healing (New York: Bantam Books, 1990), pp. 57-76.

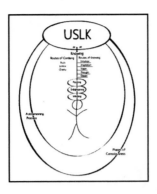

CHAPTER 3   THE "I" GRAM

All of life is in process, breathing, pulsating, moving, changing. Likewise, in life, the "I" of every person is moving constantly in processes.   Some of the results of the dynamic processes in which human beings engage can be seen: a pie, a poem, a handshake, a smile. However, the processes themselves, the reasoning, intuiting, and loving that preceded those results cannot be seen. If the invisible movings of the "I" could be frozen in place, as in a photograph, this would allow an observer to identify qualities and features of the subject, the "I".

Imagine for a moment a large, blank page in the front of a room. There is a presenter who says, "Where did life and all that supports it come from?"

Some say that the universe sprang from a 'Big Bang', but what was it that caused the 'Big Bang'?   And if the cause of that could be known, then what was the cause of that cause? Using the tool of reason alone, philosophical argument has shown that logically there has to be a 'First Cause, in itself uncaused'.

On the blank page an oval is drawn and the presenter writes within it,

Universal Source of Life and Knowledge

to represent the First Cause from a philosophical perspective, as the origin of all life and all knowledge, the source of animation of the human being.

The Universal Source of Life and Knowledge (USLK) is the beginning point of a diagram that serves as a blueprint for parts and processes in the human being. This blueprint is called the "I" Gram. It shows those components of every person which are present from conception until death, those which cannot be seen, heard or felt and those which can be seen, heard and felt. There is a drama that unfolds when the "I" Gram is drawn.

Touching and connected to that oval representing the source of life and knowledge is the metaphysical **"I"**. From the moment of conception, the "I" of the person is in a state of knowing called **"I" Knowing**. Beginning in the Universal Source of Life and Knowledge, a straight line is drawn through the "I" downward. This simple direct line represents **esca**, that moving power in every human being to take action in living life on a day to day, hour to hour, minute to minute basis. The line depicting esca is drawn straight down through a stick figure all the way to the tips of the fingers and the tips of the toes. This stick figure represents the physical body of the human being. As the line is being drawn into the fingertips and the toe tips, it is possible to begin to grasp the reality of the metaphysical moving that animates every cell of the human being.

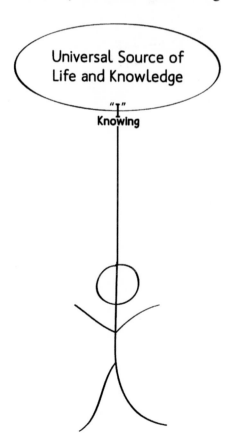

This diagram locates the source of the "I" in the USLK, but the metaphysical "I" itself, is not bound to one location. The "I" is present in the electromagnetic aura surrounding the body; it is outside the body; and it is in every cell of the body. The "I" is not bound by time and space, except as it is located in the living cells of the human body.

Located below "I" Knowing and to the right of the straight line representing esca, the presenter of the "I" Gram writes: **Routes of Knowing.**

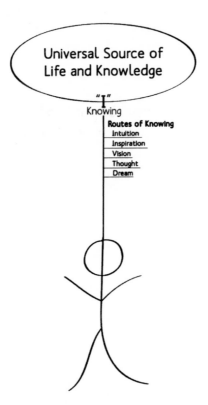

Routes of knowing are tools given to the human being for intellectual work. As life unfolds, these five tools help the person come to understand more of that knowing and to act in light of it. These routes are:

Intuition – the knowing without proof of knowing

Inspiration – the breathing in of non-concrete reality to bring something to fruition

Vision – the working with the realities of the past which become the incubator in which realities of the future form

Thought – that rational faculty of the human being which harnesses the essence of things in meaningful order

Dream- simultaneous metaphysical and physical reality; the linking of the abstract meaning and understanding of experiences with the concrete reality of day to day living.

Each human life is begun and sustained through a set of complex relationships with others. The touchstone for establishing harmonious relationships with others is that part of "I" Knowing which knows the absolute values of Truth, Justice and Charity. On the diagram, beneath "I" Knowing and to the left of the esca line, the presenter now writes: **Routes of Cordising,** which represent the means for human beings to observe Truth, Justice and Charity in all the actions they take. *Cordis,* is the Latin word for "of or from the heart". Therefore, Routes of Cordising are pathways for moving "from the heart". For example, being honest is a pathway in the observation of truth and being fair is a pathway in the observation of justice. Compassion and kindness are examples of pathways that can be used in the observation of charity, which is love in any form.

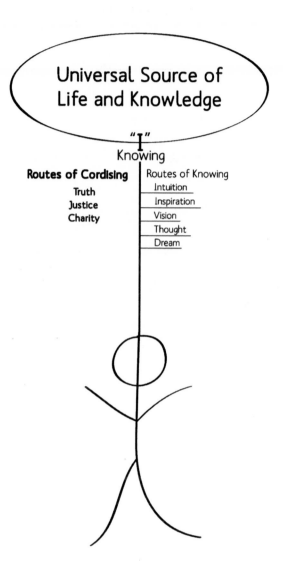

Overlaying the esca line, in a centered position, the presenter now draws three ellipses of equal size, stacked one on top of the other. They are labeled in descending order as the pooling process, the enlightening process, the minding process. **The Pooling Process** is defined as the storehouse of all that a human being experiences in living life. It is here that the results of the processes of all one's living are held: the results of intuition, inspiration, vision, thought, dream; the results of all learning; memories, and the outcomes of other actions that occur in the visible and invisible parts of human beings. As amazing as it may seem, nothing that a human being experiences is ever lost. It is in the pooling process that decisions are made. As experiences are compared to one another, or information from one experience is combined with information from another experience, a decision is formed.

The Enlightening Process is characterized by sudden bursts of clarity about life, life situations or a conceptualization of a specific quality. Enlightening represents a shift in one's understanding, where things are perceived in a new light, "Aha, now I see!" The placement of enlightening is under pooling because it is less abstract than the pooling process.

The Minding Process is the verbal factory, or library, for the selection and organization of words as human beings convey their thoughts. It is here that a person organizes actions following decisions made in the pooling process. It is here that decisions are worded for eventual expression. The minding process occurs immediately before a person speaks words or takes actions. Of all the abstract processes in self animate, the minding process is the closest to being concrete.

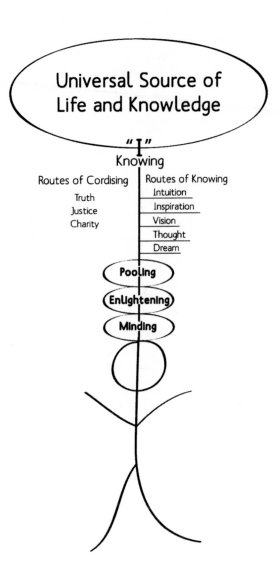

Now the presenter draws two ovals, one inside the other, both of which start with the USLK and encircle the entirety of what has been described so far, then connect back to the USLK.

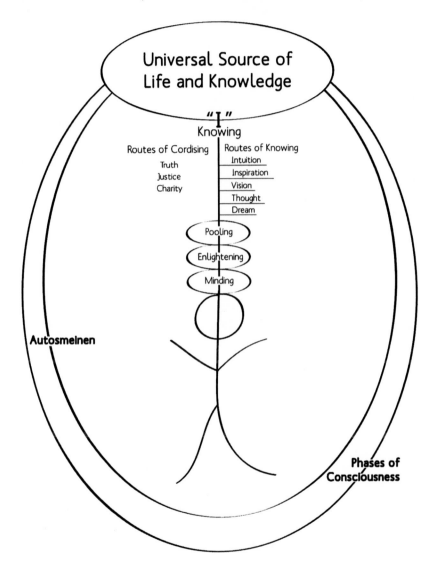

The presenter points to the inner of the two ovals: **Autosmeinen** is derived from the word, *autos*, Greek for "self", and *meinen*, Dutch for "meaning", and depicts the "meaning to self" in each person. Each person's unique piece of meaning comes from the source of all meaning contained in the Universal Source of Life and Knowledge and this piece of meaning is different from person to person. The oval of autosmeinen encompasses all that goes into living life because a human being references each moment of life from the perspective of this unique piece of meaning.

The presenter points to the remaining, outer, oval. The **Phases of Consciousness** depict the locus of control that every person has in regard to every action taken in living life. In the phases of consciousness, the person controls both seen and unseen actions, whether intellectual, physiological, spiritual or excitational in nature. The four phases of consciousness are: **volitional,** the willing of an action; **intentional**, the motivations, intentions, desires and purposes that precede an action; **attentional**, the point of one's concentration and awareness; and **overt actional**, the focus on a word or action immediately preceding the speaking of the word, or the carrying out of the action, the final surveillance of self before omission or commission of an action. The oval representing the phases of consciousness touches the Universal Source of Life and Knowledge, which is the source of consciousness in a human being. This oval then extends to surround all of the parts of the "I" Gram. It is through the phases of consciousness that "I" Knowing controls all actions and aspects of "my Self". No action can be taken without the consent of the will.

The large page at the front of the room is nearly filled with the "I" Gram, just two other components remain to be presented.

All of the concepts from the Universal Source of Life and Knowledge through the minding process and phases of consciousness, are animate or "of spirit" in nature, that is, they are invisible, inaudible and intangible. They are known as the **Self Animate** of the human being. The stick figure represents the physical body and all of its functions. This material *corpus* can be seen, heard and felt and is known as the **Self Corporeal** of the human being. Actions taken in self corporeal are the result of that moving power, esca, which comes from the Universal Source of Life and Knowledge and moves in all the components of self animate. In reality, **self animate-corporeal** is all one and cannot be separated. It is depicted here as separate components in order that this bi-dimensional aspect of the whole person can be grasped. Moving in esca is the sum total of all the visible and invisible movings in a human being.

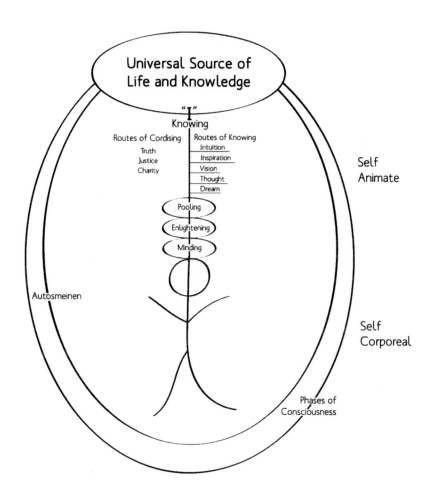

The presenter looks up at the page, now filled with the simple illustration called the "I" Gram which depicts breathing, pulsating, changing, moving, human life. There is a suspended moment of silence, then the Presenter looks at her hands in wonder and slowly moves each finger, one at a time. She pauses a moment, gently clasps both hands together, then bows her head and takes her seat.

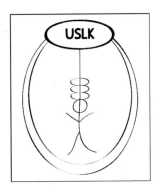

CHAPTER 4   UNIVERSAL SOURCE OF LIFE AND KNOWLEDGE

The sound and sight of water bubbling up from the ground awed and amazed us. After a three day journey following our creek through the woods we had arrived at its source! Our eyes at last beheld the spring that sustained so much in the life of our village; but my mind wanted to go farther. I wondered, "How far under the earth's crust could I trace the source of this spring? Perhaps it flows from a huge aquifer. . . If so, where did all that water come from?. . . " Each answer raised more questions. As surely as we had followed the course of our creek, my mind followed a path marked by ". . . And where did that come from? . . ."

The Question and the Questioner

And where did that come from?. . . Where did life come from?. . . Where did human beings come from?....Where did that moving power to take action in life come from?. . . Where did the cosmos and all that supports life come from? Human beings have pondered such questions for millennia. The answers have been formed by individuals and shaped by their oral histories, cultural traditions, religions and sciences. In this chapter the authors explore the reach of reason, the first tool of all the sciences, in discovering an answer.

Modern telescopes allow astronomers and physicists to see stars at greater and greater distances. The light received on earth from these distant stars was actually produced eons ago, thus allowing scientists to travel many light years back in time. The data they gathered describes conditions present as the cosmos began to form and expand. Theories proposed from this data come closer and closer to the beginning of the cosmos, tracking the emergence of elementary particles and forms of energy. That which existed <u>before</u> the very first spark of energy came into being is a mystery beyond the limits of the physical sciences to describe because there was no matter, no motion, no time for their instruments to read. Reason, which is fundamental to all science, can be used to take this query further. Reason extends beyond the limits of man-made instruments and says that something cannot come from nothing.

How far can the tool of reason take a person in the search for the ultimate source of the universe? Using intellect, human beings seek the ultimate reasons, causes and principles of things. As a part of this quest, physical scientists use reason to explain why things are as they are and why events happen as they do. Methods of research restrict discoveries to a cause close to the matter under investigation. For example, the law of gravity is limited to describing the force of attraction that causes objects to fall toward the ground. Why is there such a force as gravity? Why can it be described with such mathematical exactness? Why is there such order in the universe and where did it come from? These questions lead beyond the scope of physics and math to the first science, philosophy. "Since reason is an adequate instrument of true knowledge in the discovery and assignment of proximate causes, why should reason not be capable of reaching farther and of discovering the ultimate cause or causes of the physical world? So long as philosophy argues from the same physical world and uses the same first principles as ordinary science does, the competency of reason must be accepted in both."[1]

First Principles

As the questioner begins to reason out an answer to the ultimate question, "And where did that come from?" certain philosophical concepts and principles provide a foundation for discovering truth. Although an in-depth look at these ideas is beyond the scope of this book, it is helpful to show a brief sketch of the territory reason must traverse as it reaches for an answer.

There are self-evident truths that provide a basic foundation for sound reasoning and a point of reference when one gets lost in an intellectual "forest." They are called self-evident because they can be proven by their own luminosity and by the absurdities that follow their denial. The following four statements contain self-evident truths related to finding an answer to the question at hand, "And where did that come from?"

I exist. If I deny my own existence, then who is it that is saying, "I do not exist"?

Reality exists. The sun and the stars, the moon and the earth, all beings living and non-living and all the forces that produce change in the natural world exist. They exist objectively, whether or not they are perceived or understood subjectively, by any one human being.

Whatever happens or becomes must have a cause for its happening or becoming.

I can know truth. I can reason validly. If I say I cannot know truth and reason validly, I present that statement as true and an expression of valid thought.

It is in the nature of human beings to seek knowledge by discovering and discerning the truth about reality. Formally considered, truth is absolute and thus unchanging. It exists objectively, outside human discovery or understanding of it. A person's subjective discernment of truth exists in degrees as he or she may gain clearer and fuller understanding of it. Certainty develops when truth is manifested through <u>objective</u> evidence that an assertion is true. Reasoning involves a series of processes used to discern truth and develop certainty. As reasoning becomes more abstract, the process of inference allows one to move from certain truths already known to another truth distinct from these, but necessarily following them. In order to arrive at accurate conclusions, one must proceed from valid premises and follow the rules of logic. Through the use of reason, people are able to transcend the level of sense perception and arrive at conclusions that reach beyond those perceived by the senses. Biologists, geologists and physicists begin with their data to conclude to events which may have happened in the far distant past. They did not perceive these events. They reasoned to them, seeking truth. **This is a process similar to that which is being used right now.**

The truth of that which ultimately caused the world to exist is not self-evident. Can this answer be found by reasoning from 'the reality of the world" (something better known) to that which caused it to exist (something less well known)?

And Where Did That Come From ?

The principle of causality provides the seeker with the first stepping stone to finding an answer. "Every effect must receive its being from a cause; and the reality of the effect must proceed from the cause, because no one/no thing can give what he/it does not have...... Inherent in the concept of causality is the idea that the reality of an effect manifests in some manner the reality of its cause." [2] For example, the reality of solar light and heat (effects) is manifested by the activity of gases present in the sun (cause). "My" body carries traits caused by "my" parents, grandparents, great grandparents and so on. In like manner, whatever caused the universe to exist must be manifested in it in some aspect; therefore, it should be possible to reason logically from the existence of the world to the existence of its cause.

Philosophers have developed different proofs that use a process of reasoning to demonstrate the existence, nature and actions of a source for the universe. A philosophical proof is "a valid argument starting from true premises that yields the conclusion." [3] There are eight traditional proofs. Each one starts from a different point to reason to its conclusion. These are the proofs from sufficient reason, efficient causality, motion, design, conscience, universal consensus, practical consequences, and impossible alternative. Three of these proofs, sufficient reason, efficient causality, and conscience, follow in a brief form, based on the work of Paul Glenn.[4]

The argument from sufficient reason states that each thing must have a sufficient reason for existing. A sufficient reason is one that is complete enough to explain why something exists. This reason will be found either in the thing itself or in some other thing. If the reason for existence is found in the existing thing itself, then this thing is so perfect that it involves existence in itself; it must exist and cannot be non-existent; existence is of its very essence: it is a self-existent thing. Such a thing is called necessary. On the other hand, a thing which does not involve in itself the necessity for existence is called non-necessary or contingent. The sufficient cause for the existence of all contingent things is some other thing. If these things are contingent, then they must be caused by some other thing. An example of contingent things is the egg laid by the chicken, which came from an egg, which came from . . . and . . . chickens ultimately came from the elementary particles, carbon, hydrogen, oxygen, minerals. . . a first spark of energy. . . Whatever science proposes as the origin, the question has to be asked, "And where did that come from?" Logically, this dependency of contingent things cannot be an endless chain; at the beginning of it there must be a necessary being that is self-existent. Since the things we see around us here on earth and in the cosmos are contingent things (for they change and appear and disappear, which would be impossible if they had to exist), we rightly conclude that the world and all things in it cannot justify their existence without an appeal to other being and ultimately, necessary being.

The argument from efficient causality states that every contingent thing is efficiently caused or produced. If the efficient cause of a thing is itself the effect of a further cause, then that further cause must be sought. The chain of cause and effect cannot be endless. The sane mind refuses to accept the possibility of an endless series of links beginning nowhere. Likewise it would be unscientific to refuse to carry the quest of causes back to the beginning. Reason says that something cannot come from nothing. The use of reason leads to the necessity of a <u>first</u> cause. In order to be the first cause, it cannot be the effect of any other cause. A first cause, itself uncaused must exist. This first cause, uncaused, must be a necessary being, that is, a being that is so perfect that it must exist and cannot be non-existent.

Across the centuries and great variations in human cultures, there is evidence of the existence of conscience in human beings - the knowing that some actions are right and others are wrong. Philosophers call this innate knowing, the moral law. Simply stated, the moral law is to do good and avoid evil. Although persons may violate the moral law, they cannot be ignorant of it. Universal moral convictions that do not change provide evidence that human beings have knowledge of the moral law. For example, a world where murder is universally recognized as good and theft as virtuous is unthinkable. When human laws and customs distort or violate the moral law, they, too, are evidence that those people recognize the <u>existence</u> of good and evil. However badly individuals and societies misapply the moral law, they still are working within the moral framework that right and wrong <u>exist</u>. For example, genocide is often justified by claiming those being murdered are not fully human beings, and therefore such action is right and good. Such a violation, horrific as it is, still serves to prove that human beings have always and everywhere recognized the existence of right and wrong, the existence of the moral law. That it is distorted, violated, misapplied or ignored does not erase its existence. Rather, such distortions show that there is a law there to distort. Where there is knowledge of such a law, there must be a source for it, a lawgiver and ultimately, a first lawgiver that is distinct from human nature and superior to it, who requires changeless and absolute adherence to good and changeless avoidance of evil.

So, how far can reason take us in answering the question, "And where did that come from?" It can take us to the place of stating with certitude there must be a necessary being, a first cause, itself uncaused and a first lawgiver. Reason also says that all of the motion and change ever present in the universe must be produced by something and ultimately must originate in a prime mover, itself unmoved. The intricate order and balance necessary for the smallest particle or the largest galaxy to exist provide evidence of a grand design for the world. Design must have its first cause, a first designer.

The design of the cosmos points to the reality "...that the world is really a 'universe.' Astrophysics has established the fact that the stars and the earth consist of the same chemical elements and are governed by the same mechanical, chemical and physical laws throughout; the world is a *coordinated system*, a totality of beings united together into a real *universe, a cosmos.* Since this involves a unified plan of construction and of activity, the changes and developments in the universe point very definitely to *One Being* as the agent responsible for the actuality acquired anywhere throughout the vast expanse of the present cosmos as we know it."[5]

Universal Source of Life and Knowledge

In the theory of moving in esca, the Universal Source of Life and Knowledge (USLK) is the necessary being, the first cause, uncaused; the first lawgiver, the prime mover, unmoved; the first designer. The six words, Universal Source of Life and Knowledge, name a philosophical concept and well reasoned conclusion that answers the ultimate question, ". . .And where did that come from?"

Universal is from the Latin, *universalis*. This is a combination of two root words: *unus,* 'one' plus *vertere,versum,* 'to turn.' Literally then, *universalis* is 'turned into one, combined whole.' It is defined as: "1. Including or covering the whole or all, either collectively or distributively. 2. Of or pertaining to the universe; present everywhere or in all. In logic and philosophy, *universal* implies reference to everyone without exception in the class, category or genus considered."[6]

The universal essence contained in the necessary being, the first cause, the first lawgiver, the prime mover, the first designer is **that without which nothing can be**. The essential note that applies universally to each of these philosophical conclusions is **that which had no beginning**. Each proof represents a different approach the intellect has made to grasp one reality: the universal source. "In the philosophical perspective of multiple reasonings, it will always come back to the need for 'that which is' to have come from a single oneness."[7] Though many explanations for causes of 'all that is' can be given, only a cause that is universal, that applies to all the phenomena of reality as grasped by the senses and the intellect, can satisfy the question, "And where did that come from?"

Source is derived from Latin and French roots that denote to lift, to spring up or rise. The noun forms denote a spring or 'the place where a watercourse springs from the ground.'[8] *Source* is defined as "Any thing or place from which something comes, arises or is obtained; origin."[9] Webster's Dictionary notes that *source* often applies to the point where something springs into being; but since this is often dubious, the term is frequently modified in order to add to its clarity. This comment explains the necessity of the use of *universal source* to identify that from which all else has sprung.

_Of_ has an ancient ancestry going back to the prehistoric Indo-European preposition, *ap,* 'origin' or 'removal.'[10] Its definitions include:1.) "Used to indicate derivation, origin or source. 2.) Possession, connection, association."[11]

Life is derived from the prehistoric German verb, *lib,* which denotes 'remain, be left, continue.' The connection between 'remaining' and 'life' is thought to be the notion of being 'left alive after a battle.'[12] *Life* is defined as

1.) Quality or character distinguishing an animal or plant from inorganic or from dead organic bodies, which is especially manifested by metabolism, growth, reproduction, and internal powers of adaptation to environment. 2.) The vital force whether regarded as physical or spiritual, the presence of which distinguishes organic from inorganic matter. 3.) Existence, especially conscious existence; conceived as a quality of the soul or as the soul's nature and being. [13]

As things move in and out of existence, life can almost be defined in terms of change and motion. The 'vital force' causing such movement can be described and explained in many ways, but ultimately there must be a source for this animating principle, a source for your life and mine. Since this book presents a theory about human beings and that moving power each person has to take action in life, it is important to recognize from where that moving power came. The origin of that moving power and the origin of life is the First Cause, itself uncaused, here called *the universal source of life*.

Knowledge is defined as, fact or state of knowing; perception of fact or truth; clear and certain mental apprehension. [14] Although knowledge is gained throughout life from experience and study, the 'state of knowing' in a human being is larger than acquired facts, truths, principles or skills. The order, design and purpose evident everywhere in the cosmos and in all forms of life could not have been manifested if each being or thing did not have a means of carrying out its part in the overall design. In human beings, this larger state of knowing provides such a means. It includes the knowing of the moral law and other dimensions of knowing that will be explored at length in the following chapters. [15]

Because such knowing is a universal aspect of human nature, it, too, must come from that one source. That oneness from which life and this state of knowing in the human being arose is called the

Universal Source of Life and Knowledge (USLK). As a philosophical concept, those six words represent some aspects of a source of life that can be arrived at through reasoning. According to their beliefs, persons give names to the USLK. Through contemplation, meditation, prayer and revelation people go beyond the limits of reason to develop their faith. The understanding gained through such avenues contributes to the field of theology. The theory of moving in esca "accommodates any and all positions and views in regard to the <u>ORIGIN</u> of the 'I', to the source of life, moving in esca, and the Self." [16] The Universal Source of Life and Knowledge is the origin of "I" Knowing and all of the processes in human beings.

There are more aspects of the nature of the Universal Source of Life and Knowledge that can be arrived at through the use of reason. [17] For example, in the course of proving its existence, general things about the nature of USLK were evident. It was shown that the Universal Source of Life and Knowledge is **self-existent** and subject to no causation. Because of this fact nothing can be added or taken away from the USLK, for such addition or subtraction would be effects and thus imply causation. Since USLK is the First Being (which produces all other beings), there is nothing outside of such a being that can be added to it; and there is no cause that can affect it by subtraction. Nor can it be said that self-causation could account for possible additions or subtractions to such a being; self-causation is a contradiction in terms. A being which cannot be increased or decreased and which is itself the cause of all other perfection or being is absolutely without bounds or limits. Such a being is **infinite**.

There is only one Universal Source of Life and Knowledge and it is without equal; it is **unique**. There cannot be a plurality of infinite beings. Should there be two such beings, there would be a distinction, a line of demarcation, a <u>limit</u> between them. This line would distinguish the perfections of Being A from those of Being B. Being A would lack the distinct qualities of Being B and thus could conceivably have them added to it. But an infinite being can have nothing added to it, thus Being A and Being B must really be one being; or neither A nor B is infinite. There can be only one infinite being.

Since the Universal Source of Life and Knowledge is infinite, it is **simple**, uncomposed, free from the limitation of dependence upon parts. Every bodily being is made of a number of limited parts. A part as such is limited; but USLK is without limits. USLK is **spirit**: a non-bodily, infinite substance.

Other attributes also follow from the attribute of infinity, such as, changeless, eternal, immeasurable, all-knowing, all-wise, all-powerful. All of these perfections of the USLK are one with another and one with the undivided essence and nature of the Universal Source of Life and Knowledge.

Philosophically the actions of USLK upon the world can be described as **producing**, **preserving** and **governing** it. The action of producing the world is called *creation,* which is the production of a thing hitherto not existing, without use of any subject matter from which it is made. That which is created relies on the power that created it to continue existence - to preserve its existence. Because the Universal Source of Life and Knowledge is boundless wisdom, it does nothing without purpose. Thus the world must have been created for a purpose. The infinite wisdom of the USLK must have arranged a means for accomplishing its purpose and must apply these means to their function. To arrange means and apply them is to govern; therefore USLK governs the world. Such control or governance is evident in the laws of nature which are witnessed by all creatures as a matter of daily experience. The discoveries of science reveal more and more of the intricate complexities of such laws. As human beings grapple with achieving happiness, the moral law acts as a lighthouse. It illuminates obstacles and dangers to avoid, as well as lights a path for the doing of good. The Universal Source of Life and Knowledge has thus provided for the cosmos and all creatures a means to achieve its purpose in producing the world.

...My mind followed the arduous path of reason and logic to answer the question, "And where did that come from?" At last I arrived at the Universal Source. I felt awed by the necessity of its existence and amazed by the logical reality of its nature.

Just as my eyes and ears could sense only a small part of the stream's path at a time, so too my intellect could grasp only one idea at a time. I had arrived step by step at the truth that something must exist that was beyond the powers of my senses or intellect to fully grasp. And yet somehow I knew that the Cause that gave me the ability to reach so far with my mind, must have also provided other means of knowing It than the marvelous, though limited powers of my senses and intellect. A truth so big as this must have many paths to it.

---

[1] Bittle, Celestine N., God and His Creatures, THEODICY (Milwaukee: The Bruce Publishing Co., 1953), p. 38

[2] Bittle, Celestine, Reality and the Mind, EPISTEMOLOGY (Milwaukee: The Bruce Publishing Co., 1944), p.68.

[3] Oxford University Dictionary, 1994, p. 306.

[4] Glenn, Paul J., Sociology, a Class Manual in the Philosophy of Human Society (St. Louis: B. Herder Book Co., 1941), pp. 19-45.

[5] Bittle, Celestine N., The Doman of Being, ONTOLOGY (Milwaukee: The Bruce Publishing Co., 1939), p. 108.

[6] Webster's New Collegiate Dictionary (Springfield, Mass.: G. and C. Merriam Co., 1961)

[7] Kinlein, M. Lucille, from a Learning Session (Homer, Alaska: August 25, 2002)

[8] Ayto, John, Dictionary of Word Origins (New York: Little, Brown and Company, Arcade Publishing, 1990), p. 490.

[9] Random House Dictionary of the English Language, The Unabridged Edition. Stein, Jess (editor-in-chief) (New York: Random House, 1967)

[10] Ayto, John, op. cit., p. 371.

[11] Random House Dictionary, op. cit.

[12] Ayto, John, op. cit., p. 323.

[13] Webster's New Collegiate Dictionary, op. cit.

[14] Random House Dictionary, op. cit.

[15] See Chapters 3, 4, 5 and 6.

[16] Kinlein, M. Lucille, Moving That Power Within, (Minneapolis: National Center of Kinlein, 1985), p. 39

[17] Glenn, Paul J., op cit, pp. 36-43.

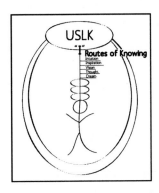

CHAPTER 5   ROUTES OF KNOWING IN PROCESS

Every living thing finds its good in the activity proper to it and the exercise of rationality is the activity proper to human beings.[1]

In order to grasp the significance of routes of knowing, one must begin with the state of the human being called "I" Knowing. The Universal Source of Life and Knowledge is the origin of "I" Knowing and all of the invisible, intangible, non-physical life processes in the human being flow from "I" Knowing. In the theory of moving in esca, these silent movings are called, collectively, "processes in self-animate".

As life is lived, the person comes to understand more and more of what is contained within "I" Knowing. Five of the processes which are instrumental in gaining this understanding, are called Routes of Knowing. The routes, which are named Intuition, Inspiration, Vision, Thought and Dream, are some of the tools for reasoning and for intellectual work of all kinds. These processes help the person come to understand more of the knowing given to every human being at the moment of conception and to act in light of it. Knowing is the process of perceiving and understanding fact or truth with clarity and certainty. The routes of knowing are used for accessing that knowing to gain further knowledge over time.

Human beings are moving in these processes all of the time and may engage these tools deliberately or not, with awareness or not. Each of the five routes of knowing: intuition, inspiration, vision, thought and dream, is described in the sections that follow.

SECTION A: THE INTUITIONARY PROCESS

A mother is standing at the kitchen counter preparing food while her toddler naps in a nearby bedroom. Suddenly, the mother has an urgent, compelling inner knowing: Johnny's in danger. She rushes to the bedroom to check on Johnny. Upon entering the room, the mother finds the child teetering on the window ledge, the window wide open and the screen gone...............

How did the mother know that her child was in danger? How do these common expressions: "gut feeling", "mother's intuition", "I just knew...", relate to the mother's experience? The inner process that best describes these human experiences and expressions is the Intuitionary Process. It is the first of the five processes in the Routes of Knowing.

What is the Intuitionary Process?

The word intuition comes from the Latin root, *intuitio*: regarding or looking at. One dictionary definition is: the direct perception of truth, independent of any reasoning process.[2] In the theory of moving in esca, the definition of the intuitionary process is, knowing without proof of knowing. The result of the intuitionary process is an intuition. To understand the process more fully, the definition can be broken down into two smaller parts: knowing and proof.

Knowing and knowledge are not the same. Knowledge is a body of facts accumulated in the course of time.[3] Knowing is a state of being, given at the moment of conception when life is breathed into the human being. What is this knowing? Part of it involves knowing about life and its purpose.   Part of it involves ways of acting and being in accomplishing that purpose. Part of it involves ways of acting and being as one faces the complexities in living life.

Regarding proof: In the process of acquiring facts about the world, that is, gaining knowledge, the facts provide evidence that either supports that knowledge or contradicts it. Proof is the evidence supporting or affirming something unequivocally. By collecting, developing, and organizing evidence, human beings prove to themselves things about the world in which they live. This is the way that human beings gain glimpses of truth and develop a degree of certainty about what they know.

The unique feature of the intuitionary process is that the resultant knowing, called an intuition, comes with a high degree of certainty but without proof. The certainty both anchors and complements the very abstract nature of the process itself. In fact, the process has a laser-like quality that requires no analysis and is clean of attachments to anything such as tentativeness, uncertainty and doubt. Intuitions can be about anything of importance. Human beings are moving in their intuitionary processes all of the time. Most people can remember their specific intuitions quite clearly. Intuitions have the additional characteristics of singularity, completeness, and clarity.

The Person, Moving in the Intuitionary Process

The most important internal conditions necessary for beneficial use of intuition are openness and trust. Johnny's mother could have ignored her intuition by telling herself: he couldn't possibly be in danger; he's asleep. Instead, using her intuition as a guide to action, she checked on her son.

Once a person has received an intuition, it is important to give it high priority. For example, Johnny's mother puts all other action in a holding pattern while she pays attention to the knowing contained in that intuition and responds to it. As the mother sees her toddler on the window ledge, there is integration of the original intuition with other movings in self animate so as to identify how best to act in light of that intuition. Should she grab Johnny from the window ledge? Should she speak in a low tone and call his name? Should she call Johnny in her "I mean business" voice?

While all human beings come equipped with the intuitionary process, the content that flows through it is unique to each person. Personal views, beliefs and experiences affect the person moving in the intuitionary process as does previous experience. Thus, Johnny's mother will move uniquely in responding to her intuition, according to her knowing of herself, her child and the big picture.

Learning to recognize and trust one's intuition is a process that begins early in life. A child may receive an intuition and then observe that time confirms its accuracy. Often there is an immediate cellular response. The phrase "I had a gut feeling" illustrates this phenomenon. Another way human beings come to recognize and trust their intuitions is by experiencing the consequences of ignoring them. Most adults have had the experience of ignoring an intuition and regretting it later.

The act of a person moving in the intuitionary process, is good in and of itself. It exists to bring benefit to self and others. Anything that suggests or demands action that is harmful to self or to others is contrary to observing truth, justice and charity and would not be an intuition.

There is a difference between the "I" of the person, receiving an intuition as a result of moving in the intuitionary process and other concepts such as fate, karma and foretelling. Life is full of surprises and unexpected adventures. No one can predict the future with certainty. More importantly, every action a person takes requires an act of the will and has a result. These factors lead to the logical conclusion that the future of every human being is built through actions taken in the present.

The mother moves swiftly to her child and lifts him from harm's way. As he squirms in her arms in his beginning journey toward independence, she smiles and breathes a sigh of relief. She cannot know what lies ahead for her son, but she has affirmed to herself, the importance of paying attention to that inner voice of intuition.

SECTION B: THE INSPIRATIONARY PROCESS

Colour has taken hold of me; no longer do I have to chase after it. I know that it has hold of me forever. That is the significance of this blessed moment. (Artist Paul Klee on a visit to Tunis in 1914)

A breath inspired fills the lungs with air and fills the heart with a sense of... This Moment... as the artist translates a memory in his prose. The reader can feel his excitement of being captured by color and the importance of what he now knows.

The word inspiration comes from a Latin root *inspiratio* which is defined as: to breathe upon or into. In the theory of moving in esca, inspiration is defined as the breathing-in of nonconcrete reality to bring something to fruition. It is the result of "I" moving in the second Route of Knowing, the Inspirationary Process, the process of forming "knowings" into a cohesive whole or unit, mistiness sculptured into recognizable ideas.

Breathing-in is an active process that enables the very cells of a person to take things in. *Nonconcrete reality* refers to intangible, immaterial, abstract qualities involving truth, justice and charity as they permeate all things...the truth of beauty, the truth of color. The breathing in of non-concrete reality enables the person to see new truths in relationship to anything or to see old truths in a new way. The second part of the definition, *to bring something to fruition* describes the purpose of the process of inspiration, to bring something to accomplishment, attainment or realization.

Inspiration is the result of a process that exists in every human being and the "I" of every person is moving in the inspirationary process all of the time. But how does this moving bear fruit?

Certain subprocesses set the stage for the forming of an inspiration. There is a situation, puzzle, or goal that is a focal point. This focus is one that has a significance, influence or effect that is important to the person involved. Listening to oneself, trusting oneself and being willing to let go of previously held views or thoughts can help a person open up to new possibilities, however hazy. Moving in other processes in self animate, the person may gather and organize information and apply some reasoning to the matter at hand. When these movings do not produce the desired outcome, an inspiration may form. The following two accounts provide examples of the process leading up to and following an inspiration and illustrate the feature of uniqueness of each person.

> I had been working on the project for months, trying one approach after another to find the right structure for chapters in the textbook I was writing. I read similar textbooks, consulted with other authors, and spoke with my editor. Nothing seemed to be just right but something very vague was hovering there. I kept pushing but nothing further came. Finally I decided to take a break and went for a walk on the beach. As I looked at the clear blue water on one side and the velvet green mountains on the other, the vague hazy shape that had been so near yet so far began to come closer and to take on a more clearly defined form. Fearing that it might slip away from me, I paused to absorb the new possibility and thought: Yes, this might just work and it surely is worth a try. Later, I went back to work and was able to turn this new possibility into chapters that greatly strengthened the book.

In this account, the limits of data collection and reasoning were reached and there was an impasse. The person attempted to resolve the impasse by working with various pieces of the situation or puzzle, but these efforts did not bear fruit. Eventually, there was an acknowledgement and acceptance of the impasse and a letting go both of the internal tension surrounding the matter and of attempts to bring it to fruition. Thus there was no further struggle and a state of relaxed alertness was present. If asked, the person might describe the matter as being "on the back burner". It is during this time (which may last for hours or days) that an inspiration may come as that vague and hazy rough draft of an action to be taken or a goal to be accomplished. The inspiration is not a piece or small part, but more of a whole action or goal, though it is vague. The temptation is great to resume working on the matter immediately, but it is most helpful to absorb the inspiration as fully as possible first. Later, once absorption is complete, work on the object of inspiration can continue with more concrete, practical results. As the writer resumed working on the matter, there was more clarity and a growing confidence that she was on the right track, though there was still plenty of room for trial and error.

The second account is another example of "I" moving in the inspirationary process.

> The student asked me a question and there was something in it that had never been asked before in that way in more than forty years of teaching. I paused, took a deep breath and began to answer the question. Afterwards, I asked for the answer to be read back to me because I did not know what I had just said. I realized that I had spoken from my inspirationary process. As my response to the question was read back to me, I realized that there were no corrections or additions to be made.

In this account, the teacher first identified the question as containing something different from the many other questions she had answered in more than forty years of teaching. As she paused and took a deep breath, the effect on the cells in her body was an opening up to all of her knowledge about teaching, students, this student, the content of the question, the way in which it was asked and how it would have to be answered. None of this knowledge could be grasped by the senses. This is an example of the breathing-in of nonconcrete reality. The teacher was so focused on bringing the results of the movings in self animate into her response that she could not recall fully what she had spoken, and asked for her words to be read back. It was then that she judged her response to the question to be accurate and complete.

These accounts show also that inspiration is not a generalized state; it exists in regard to something specific, an action to be taken or a goal to be accomplished. In contrast to intuition which is characterized by certainty about what action to take or which way to move, inspiration has a more fragile quality that combines shafts of clarity with parts still missing.

There is an old saying that inspiration has to be combined with perspiration in order to make anything happen. In the first account, the writer eventually had to return to the book project to put the new possibilities into the concrete form of words on a page leading to chapters. In the second example, the teacher had to provide an answer to the question the student was asking. Artist Paul Klee may be inspired to paint a masterpiece involving color yet no amount of inspiration will produce that masterpiece unless the artist picks up a paintbrush, loads it, and applies it to canvas or paper. It is in the taking of further action that inspiration is made concrete and complete.

Each human being, moving in esca, in the inspirationary process, is able to receive inspiration. Knowing how to set the stage, how to wait and pause for absorption of this breathing-in of nonconcrete reality furthers the use of this tool and allows each person to bring greater good to fruition. Writing a personal note, cooking a meal, composing music, speaking just the right words to a child, or inventing something new... all are examples of human action that brings nonconcrete reality to fruition. Woven into all aspects of everyday life, big and small, inspirations contribute to the expansion and extension of our knowledge and understanding of life.

As a breath of air enters the lungs and oxygen crosses the capillary membranes into the blood stream, every cell in the body is nourished, the fruit of which is life. Likewise, as the essence of an idea moves through the inspirationary process, a whole concept is nourished, the fruit of which is the enhancement of life.

SECTION C: THE VISIONARY PROCESS

"During that Spring, 1971, I had been giving a lot of thought to my ideas on helping people. Prior to that time, I had said to my family, to my students, to others, 'Someday I am going to open my own office.' It was unheard of at that time for a person in my field to be autonomous in a practice, but I could see that there was a gap in what the patient went to the doctor for and what would help the patient if that gap were filled. There was a vision of something lacking in regard to the person's, the patient's, perspective; the nature of that was unlimited in my vision. It was as though I could see that what would be opened up for the patient was his personal feelings, perspective of himself, what he thought he needed. I had a faint picture of what could be, but how could I make it available to the public? Gradually, the picture became clearer, and I could see a freedom for the professional and for the person seeking care, to move in mutuality for the best outcome.

On this particular afternoon, as I was correcting student papers in my office at Georgetown University, the thought came to me: 'Do it now. Open your own office for practice. Do it now.' I did not hesitate. I put down my red pencil, picked up the telephone and placed a call to a real estate agent. Within the month I had opened my office with a shingle hanging outside which read, simply, 'M. Lucille Kinlein, R.N.' "[4]

Throughout the unfolding of life, there are moments when a human being seeks a perspective that includes past, present and future. Scientists tell us that everything – from the smallest particle to the largest solar system – is moving all of the time. The fact that nothing is stationary makes change a part of living life.

We are all moving with change on a day to day basis. Seeing 'what was' and looking to 'what can be' is a part of the experience of all persons. Leaders, founders, and inventors see new possibilities in light of past realities, for people and for the world. This phenomenon is termed "vision" and it is not limited to leaders, founders and inventors. It is a process in every human being which makes it possible to gain a perspective of self in relationship to space and time. The visionary process is the third of the five processes in the Routes of Knowing in every human being.

As the "I" of the person moves in the visionary process, "...realities of the past become the incubator in which the realities of the future form."[5] There is an "embryonic, architectural"[6] quality to this process that permits a person to apprehend possibilities without defining what, where, how or when. Anything that impedes the "I" moving drops away, and there is a sense of timelessness. The only concrete aspect is something from the past, but even that becomes mist-like as it is enfolded within the visionary process. The result of these movings is vision, in the abstract. Unlike the concreteness of what the eyes see, this vision is like a very faint sketch where new connections and new applications may be seen. The seeing does not involve any kind of predicting or foretelling, but rather, a knowing of the possibility.

In order to flesh out the faint sketch of a vision, "I" Knowing moves back and forth from vision to other processes in the routes of knowing and the whole of self animate. For example, the visionary process acts as a bridge to the more concrete thoughtary process. Vision is way out there, and the person takes steps, actions, waits; going from ephemeral....to....concrete....back to ephemeral....and so on. As all of the processes in self animate-corporeal are utilized, the "I" of the person can move with a vision to make it more concrete. This usually occurs gradually over months or years. The outcome is a more defined sketch that can be built on to form detailed plans. In this way the visionary process bears fruit as it provides a glimpse of self in the dimension of time which has not yet happened....the future.

For example, a person considering retirement might engage in the visionary process, using knowledge of self in the past and present to get a view of the future. As the process unfolds, a reality of the past, "Up to now, my work has provided meaning for my life, a reason to get up and get going in the morning," and present, "What does retirement give me? Time. Ok, what do I do with this time?", becomes the incubator for nourishing a future reality, "I can't see myself playing an endless round of golf or traveling the world non-stop. I want to do something that will give meaning to this time in my life. In what activities do I find meaning? I think I'd like to do something that brings people in our community together." The idea is compelling, but other processes are necessary to fill in this faint sketch. "Maybe I could open some kind of a shop, a place where people enjoy gathering – perhaps a coffee shop or ice cream parlor", is a thought that could begin to fill in the sketch. The person, then, can move into the more concrete stages of planning how to make it happen. The initial vision may not be the eventual outcome, but it sets the stage for, and will be related to, what results.

What is absent in the visionary process are the "what-ifs" and it is this that lends a certainty to the vision. The desire to move with it becomes almost irrepressible. The person with the vision cannot put it into words. A necessary aspect of the visionary process is *waiting*. The value of the vision may not be reflected in the understanding, the acknowledgement, or even the encouragement from others. The value will be the fruit that comes as the vision unfolds into a present reality.

The tool of vision is a part of that moving power in every person to take action in living life, and therefore is, in and of itself, good. How a person uses the tool of vision affects whether benefits accrue to self and others. As each person moves in that moving power throughout life, the "I" of the person uses the tool of vision to shape a unique journey of change. These changes have born such fruit as clean water for drinking, insulated clothing to conserve body heat in cold climates, electricity to provide light and other conveniences. Through the vision of one, the eyes of many have been opened to a variety of possibilities, opportunities, challenges, and choices.

Fear and despair are the greatest enemies of the visionary process.[7] The good that can come from the fruit of the visionary process is spoiled only by any one person's intent to use it for things that are not good, and others unwilling to say "No" or "Yes". This is why the cultivation of courage and hope is so important, whether it be through the efforts of one person working alone, or the synergy of many persons uniting their efforts to make a vision real.

"What I could see was the fruit of my caring with others, and I could see the freedom I'd have to do that. What I barely glimpsed way out there in the mist, was that which would become the first new profession in 100 years...........the means required the seemingly small step of opening an office."[8]

SECTION D   THE THOUGHTARY PROCESS

"------your thought clothed with your words is uniquely you, came with you, would vanish if you vanished-------"[9]

The Metropolitan Museum of Art in New York City houses a bronze sculpture by Auguste Rene' Rodin. This larger-than-life figure is of a man, seated, with the elbow of his right arm supported on one knee and his chin resting on the back of his hand. For Rodin, beauty in art consisted in the truthful representation of inner states as depicted in this magnificent piece entitled, "The Thinker".

What is it that is so universal to thinking that all who see this sculpture comprehend its title? What is the process of thought formation? What connection does it have to the physical body? What is a thought?

A thought is the product of a nonverbal process that has identifiable elements such as a minimum of two ideas, ingredients or dimensions, which are connected. The information or material which goes into a thought can come from almost anywhere: reading a book; overhearing someone else's conversation; a classroom discussion; the ambiance of an environment. Whatever the source, the thought itself is formed in self animate, the intangible, inaudible, invisible part of every human being.

> "It is likely that no thought is ever heard in the full splendor of its pristine state."
> M. Lucille Kinlein

A thought is ethereal yet its essence is made tangible as the person speaks, writes, or signs. The fullness of a thought as first conceived in self animate can never be conveyed in its completeness to another. Some of the essence of the original thought is lost as the "I" sends the thought through the processes in self animate, then through the cells of the body and then through a mode of expression.

In its initial form, a thought is not worded. Once it is worded, the thought goes through the switchboard of the brain and through every cell in the body. If the person desires to express the thought, it will emerge through the larynx as spoken words, or as signed or written words. The importance of thoughts and the control one has over them should not be underestimated since every word a person speaks, every action a person takes and every feeling a person experiences, is preceded by a thought.

The Process of Thought Formation

The thoughtary process is defined as "engaging in abstract reasoning that harnesses the essence of things in meaningful order; the sequential processes in the formation of a thought."[10] The thoughtary process is a series of separate, unworded, intangible processes. It draws from all the other processes and sub-processes in self animate as the thought is formed. The ongoingness of all the components and processes in self animate is continuous and simultaneous and a person's focus on any particular process is constantly shifting. Therefore, the thoughtary process is going on all of the time, whether or not the focus of one's attention is on that process.

An example of deliberate focus in the thoughtary process is when one says, "Wait a minute", or "Let me think". In saying these words, a person begins the sub-processes in the thoughtary process: sensations occur in the body; metabolism drops to a lower rate; there is a calming of the heart rate and an opening of the blood vessels. A difference can be noted in the way the body feels because cellular physiology has slowed. There is a sense of the slowing of things outside the body and a slowing of things inside the body during the period of time that one is working with, "Let me think".

The complexity of moving in the thoughtary process can be described in three sequential phases:

1. The first phase is called *Selection of Essences.* Essences are selected from any of the processes in self animate and will come together to form the thought. There is a constant moving in and among all the processes in self animate as these essences are selected.
2. The second phase is called *Distillation of Essences.* The essences are honed, ordered and connected as the whole of the essence, or aspects of it, are captured to be put into the thought.
3. The third phase is called *Crystallization of Essences.* The results of Selection and Distillation are clarified in this phase. There is a lacing of the points and facets, crystallizing them into the form of a thought. As the process ends, a judgment is made of what is desired to be communicated.

The thoughtary process enables human beings to: use logic to arrive at a conclusion; engage in abstract reasoning; acquire facts; form opinions and beliefs based in reasoning; and, form judgments and conclusions using the test of reason. When combined with other processes in the human being, the thoughtary process enables us to act in a reasonable manner in the world and provides a basis for living life in accordance with the knowledge one has, balanced with the values one holds.

Control of the Thoughtary Process

Control of the thoughtary process lies in the "I" of the person moving in self animate-corporeal. The "I" always has control. Thoughts may be summoned and held, or they can be altered, diffused or stopped entirely. If it were not possible for human beings to control movings in thoughtary process, it would be hard to explain the magnificent books that have been written, the beautiful music that has been composed and the elegant art that has been accomplished.

Rodin observed human actions with the eye of one seeking to see the inner workings, which give rise to the observable acts of humankind. The posture of the man called "The Thinker" portrays a human being in a mode of contemplation, as the thoughtary process whirs within him in unworded, intangible, invisible movings.

In light of the knowledge that every word, every action, and every feeling is preceded by a thought, and every thought is under the control of the "I" of the person, human beings are the only creatures who can choose to speak, act, and feel in a particular manner. This control provides the blessing and the burden of rights, privileges, and responsibilities.

SECTION E: THE DREAMARY PROCESS

"So, Jacob left Beer-sheba and journeyed toward Haran. That night, he stopped to camp at sundown, he found a rock for a headrest and lay down to sleep, and dreamed that a staircase reached from earth to heaven, and he saw angels of God going up and down upon it."[11]

Dream is a universal experience of human beings. Recorded as early as 3100 BC by the Sumerians in Mesopotamia, dreams have held a fascination for dreamers and others up through the centuries. Jacob's dream as documented in the Bible from the book of Genesis took place about 1929 BC. The scenes that unfold during dream are replete with mystery, drama, sorrow, joy, and enlightenment. Dreaming is as natural as breathing.

Webster defines dream as a succession of images, thoughts or emotions passing through the mind during sleep; a daydream or reverie.[12] In the theory of moving in esca, dream is the fifth route of knowing and is defined as a "simultaneous physical and metaphysical reality, linking the power of the abstract with the power of the concrete, making sleep the transistor of the power."[13]

The dream state can be verified through physiological monitoring in a laboratory setting. In studies of the stages of sleep, researchers noticed lengthy and sustained *rapid eye movement,* (REM). Subjects were awakened during REM and related that they were dreaming which affirmed that dreaming takes place during sleep.

The flow of movings in *self animate-corporeal,* is affected during sleep. The intangible, invisible, inaudible abstract movings in self animate may be experienced by the dreamer as tangible, visible, audible concrete reality. This may result in tears, a rapid heartbeat, body movements, voice sounds and visual/auditory perceptions. The following brief accounts illustrate the abstract and concrete features common to dreams:

I was dreaming I saw a fire engine at a neighbor's house which had flames shooting up from the roof. Suddenly, I awoke feeling *scared.* Then I realized that the sound of the fire engine was coming from the highway.

In my dream I had to say a final good-bye to my father. When I woke up I had *tears* on my pillow.

It was a dream that I still remember to this day. I was ice-skating on a pond and I felt so free, flying through the air, noticing everything around me. When I awoke, I had a *wonderful feeling* that stayed with me a very long time.

Dream Formation

The forming of a dream begins as the "I" engages in a quiet "letting go" of all in self animate. This is followed by a calm state. As the dream begins, it has a timeless misty quality with floating threads, indicating the formation of something concrete from something abstract. The threads may be points that appear untethered resulting in a "floating over" aspect like senseless fragments. When a person awakens from such a dream and reflects upon it, there may appear to be a lack of any connections but there is always some relationship to aspects of one's life.

In contrast, tethered dreams are attached to a central point with other points around it. The central point is the attachment to something the dreamer has experienced. There is some significance related to one's life, relationships, a matter that could be resolved. Recurring dreams have the characteristic of being tethered. A person may have a recurring dream about a situation, some obligation, or some action to be taken. [14]

During sleep, the guard that protects a person in an awake state from difficult or painful experiences, relaxes or eases. This explains how nightmares occur. A nightmare in its recurring aspect would indicate the likelihood of a justified concern such as the awareness of situations, persons, animals, or natural disasters.

For this reason, it is not wise to prevent a nightmare; rather a person would benefit in working with the content of the nightmare as the following account illustrates.

Annie was four when her mother died. The grief she suffered which was never addressed in an awake state entered her dreams. The dreams were frequent and lasted for several years. In the dream, Annie found herself standing next to a square hole in the ground. When she looked down, it was very dark. Her mother was in the hole calling to her. She was unable to help her mother. Annie awoke shaking with uncontrollable tears.

The "I" of the person allowed a dream of this nature to form. After many attempts in working with the content, the dream no longer had a claim on Annie.

The content of a dream may originate from anyplace in self animate. During dream, the "I" is free to move back and forth in time and to move in any single and every single subprocess in self animate-corporeal. Still, most content comes from that place where all learning and experience is deposited, the pooling process. During dream, "I" Knowing prompts the release of contents in the pooling process and these become the subject of the dream. Since all moving in self animate-corporeal is unique in each person, the content deposited in pooling is unique. Therefore, that which is retrieved from pooling and enters a dream is unique.

Denise has been blind from birth. What she retrieved from pooling did not include the imagery of a sighted person. Yet the words she used in describing her dream contain vivid descriptions that combine information from other senses with her experience of her mother. Here is her dream as she related it.

> I dreamed about my mother. I heard her voice and I felt her gentle touch. My mother was working in a store. There were shelves of big records on one side of the store. I had a pocketbook filled with lots of money. I wanted to buy an oldies swing record. My mother turned around and found the

record I was looking for and she placed it in my hands. My mother rang up the price on a computer-like cash register. I received the change and the receipt was placed in the bag with the record. There were lines of people buying records.

Denise described her mother's movements in turning, the rustle of the plastic bags, the sound of the sneakers of people who were walking, and the jingling of change. Finally, she described her mother's touch that was so dear to her. It is important to recognize that it was not blindness that made Denise's dream unique. It is Denise who is unique.

The Role Of The Will And Dream

The feature of control is always present as a person moves through life. Since the "I" of every person is always in control of self, the will permeates all movings in all processes from the most aware level to the least aware level. Thus, the will influences every aspect of the dreamary process. The control is so strong that the "I" Knowing of a person may start, stop or change any aspect of a dream at any time.

A person may enter the dreamary process with the *intention* of finding an answer, a solution, a clarity regarding something as the following account illustrates.

Jackie was given an opportunity to change her job. It was a challenge to weigh and measure the benefits of staying in her current job with the benefits of a new position. She grappled with this before bedtime unable to come to a decision. Jackie deliberately focused on her question as she fell off to sleep. When she woke the next morning, it was clear to her that she would accept the new position.

In this account, the focus was identified and intentionally set. Distractions of the awake state did not hamper the "I" moving in the dreamary process. The results of moving in the dreamary process produced clarity and a decision was made.

Acquiescence is required not only for awareness in a dream but also for acceptance of what the dream reveals. The dreamer may choose not to remember a dream and may make an attempt to forget it. Or, a dreamer may choose to pay attention to a dream and/or to hold on to its contents.

The *exercise of choice* is possible even in a dream. Margaret's account of her dream illustrates how she responded in light of her knowing of right from wrong.

> While I was dreaming a handsome man approached and asked to have an intimate relationship. I began to think that this man is married and I couldn't do what he wanted anyway. I had to be true to myself.

The *desires* of the heart may be fulfilled in a dream as this account illustrates:

Mary's husband, Steve, died a sudden death. She did not have a chance to say good-bye. In her dream she saw Steve sitting in his favorite chair. She was conversing with him when she realized that he was not alive. Steve smiled at her as though he knew what she was thinking. It was her chance to say a final good-bye.

The "I" of Mary in her longing to see her husband, bypassed the restrictions of the awake state and acquiesced to a dream that made it possible to visit with him while at the same time recognizing the incongruity of seeing him. Some circumstances in life, such as Steve's sudden death, may not be controllable but there is always control of self in relationship to circumstances.

Dream And Meaning

What is basic to the essence of human beings is that each human being is unique at creation and that uniqueness is woven into every aspect of moving in esca. Every breath they take, every thought they have, everything cherished and loved is their very own. Like fingerprints, no two persons are identical. The uniqueness of a human being moving in the awake state and the dream state may never be fully understood but the beauty of the sameness and the differentness can be noted and appreciated.

In the dreamary process, the moving in self animate-corporeal embodies the uniqueness of the person. Therefore, logic dictates that it is not valid to say, your dream means ....! Applying generalizations to another's dream is to be avoided. Although a dreamer may be assisted in looking at a dream, only the dreamer is able to identify the *meaning* conveyed by that dream.

To answer questions about a dream, the dreamer works in the awake state in other processes that help to find it's meaning. Consider the following dream and how the thoughtary process assisted the dreamer in finding meaning.

> In one of my recurring dreams, I found myself standing outside a store where there was a steady stream of people going in and out. I was attired only in a shortie nightgown. Realizing the inappropriateness of my garb, I was surprised that no one noticed me. I was relieved; at the same time I had feelings of disappointment that no one saw me there. What did this mean?

Through working in my thoughtary process, I received enlightenment. I concluded that I wanted to feel comfortable being in front of an audience who could appreciate me. My problem, I decided, was self-consciousness. Once I identified the problem I was able to work on it. Self-consciousness was eventually replaced by self-confidence. I never had that dream again.

In a previous account, Denise related a dream that included her *mother's gentle touch*. Those few words contain what Denise experienced with her mother throughout all her life. Only she understands the meaning conveyed to her in the dream. Denise also has a recurring dream about fire in her residence. She hears a crackling noise, feels the heat and calls but no one comes to rescue her. With assistance Denise identified the reason for these dreams. She then took action to implement a change that provided a feeling of safety.

Dream is a route of knowing in every human being, helping us to come to understand what we already know. Dream unbridled brings freedom to the dreamer to explore the content of all that is stored in the pooling process. Time there is non-existent. Dreams allow the dreamer to fly through the air, be many places at the same moment, communicate with another alive in body or alive in spirit. Dream helps to solve problems, experience tender and sad or happy feelings. Dreams may also be sources of inspiration, illumination and an opening of the heart to the Universal Source of Life and Knowledge.

(All Dreams are actual accounts from persons who have given permission to use them in this chapter.)

---

[1] Aristotle. Nichomachean Ethics, Book 1. Written in 350 B.C.E. Translated by W.D. Ross.

[2] Webster's New Universal Unabridged Dictionary, DeLuxe Second Edition, New York: Simon and Schuster, 1983, page 964.

[3] IBID, page 1064

[4] Kinlein, M. Lucille from an interview 12/15/03.

[5] Kinlein, M. Lucille, Moving That Power Within, (Minneapolis, National Center of Kinlein, 1983), p. 60.

[6] Ibid, p. 60.

[7] Kinlein, M. Lucille, Routes of Knowing Course, 3/10/84.

[8] Kinlein, M. Lucille, from an interview Oct. 2003.

[9] Byatt, A.S., Possession, (New York: Vintage Books International, a division of Random House Publishers,1990), P. 219.

[10] Kinlein, M. Lucille, Moving That Power Within (Minneapolis, National Center of Kinlein, 1983), p. 62

[11] The Holy Bible, Genesis 28: 10-12.

[12] Webster's New Universal Dictionary, Deluxe Second Edition, (New York, Simon and Schuster, 1983), p. 595

[13] M. Lucille Kinlein, Moving That Power Within. (Minneapolis, National Center of Kinlein, 1983), p. 62

[14] M. Lucille Kinlein, Rita Martin, *Journal of ESCA/KINLEIN*, Vol. 6, June 1998, p. 27-32.

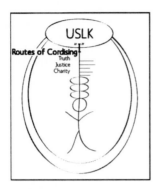

CHAPTER 6   ROUTES OF CORDISING

"It is a person of character taking action, observing truth, justice and charity that will be the force that changes the world for good."
Linda Waggoner

"Love others first, so there will be something to love about self."
M. Lucille Kinlein

Picture this scene from a true story made into an award-winning movie. The setting is Germany during World War II and the characters are a Nazi officer, Hosenfeld, and a Jewish refugee, Szpilman.

In offering to help Szpilman leave Warsaw, Officer Hosenfeld at first did not realize he was talking with a Jewish man. The officer asked the refugee what he did for a living. Learning he was a pianist, the tall, elegant officer led the unkempt, unwashed Szpilman to an out-of-tune piano in a room without windows:

When I placed my fingers on the keyboard they shook...my fingers were stiff and covered with a thick layer of dirt... I played

Chopin's Nocturne in C sharp minor...when I had finished, the silence seemed even gloomier and more eerie than before.

Officer Hosenfeld was moved with compassion and realizing the pianist was a Jew who could not leave the city, he searched and found a safe hiding place in the loft of a building. Three days later Officer Hosenfeld returned with food. Although a German commando unit moved into the building, no other soldier ever found Szpilman's refuge. [1]

Now read this newspaper article from an incident in Seattle, Washington on August 28, 2001

Egged on by Crowd, Woman Leaps from Seattle Bridge
Seattle, Washington (Reuters)– A woman leaped from a Seattle highway bridge into a ship canal Tuesday after frustrated drivers stuck in the rush-hour traffic jam she created yelled for her to jump, police said. [2]

A follow-up story several days later had these headlines and comments,

Civic Soul Searching--Ugly Ship Canal Scene
Prompts Grieving for City's Lost Civility
Seattle – 'The woman picked a lousy time to wrestle with her demons,' the Seattle Times said in an editorial. 'But despair doesn't wear a watch. The woman created an enormous traffic jam with cars backed up in almost every direction for several hours. But the city lost some of its dignity in the process...Surely congestion is not so awful that people have to lose their compassion along with their tempers.' 'This is sad evidence that we are moving from a culture of care to a culture of commerce, where obligations are so pressing on families, and time is so short that it's almost like the well of civility is beginning to run dry,' said John Kydd, a Seattle lawyer. [3]

These examples contrast the compassion and depravity evident in human actions. Regardless of circumstances - wartime, extreme poverty, traffic jams – it is the character of one individual taking action that can make a difference and influence people for good.

Character that manifests compassion and selflessness comes from observing the values of truth, justice and charity throughout life. Values that are taught to children in their formative years are more likely to become part of their character as adults.

Every action contains at least three important features: control, consequences and responsibility. As to the matter of control, it is possible for human beings to alter their behavior before an act, during an act or after an act. As to the matter of consequences, human beings are aware that their actions affect others. The combination of awareness, control and consequences leads directly to individual responsibility for any action a person takes. Every human being has a two-fold responsibility: to self and to fellow human beings. Every person can ask, "Does this action bring goodness and manifest love for my fellow human beings?" It is the choices a person makes in light of the observation or perversion of values that bring either good or harm.

Building on this relationship of control and responsibility, the profession of kinlein has identified a concept of taking action, human to human, that is active, mutual and positive. The name given to this concept is *cordising*. The Latin origin of the name is *cordis*, "from the heart." Cordising is the integration of truth, justice and charity in human actions.

Cordising Within the Person

Within the "I" Knowing of each person is a knowing of the absolute values of truth, justice and charity and the knowing of right and wrong, good and evil. This knowing is like a law within the person. In philosophy it is called the *natural law*. Although conceived with this inner knowing (also called conscience), a person spends a lifetime coming to understand it.

Truth, justice and charity are values universal to all people; they encompass all other values. *Truth* is defined as sincerity in action, character, and speech; fidelity. *Justice* is the quality of being morally just, impartial or fair; the unfailing intention of giving to everyone that which is rightly due them. *Charity* is defined as being loving and kind toward all humanity; the giving of one's self for the benefit of another. [4] The source of these values lies outside the person within the Universal Source of Life and Knowledge. In living life, persons either observe these values, or they pervert them.

What is it within a person that results in an act of care or an act of harm? It is the *will* of the person that gives consent in all actions taken. Identifying within self the reason or motive for an action taken is vital in determining if the action lines up with the values of the common good. Identifying the reason for an action requires the person to pause and examine self in order to keep a clear conscience. When one's motives in regard to an action line up with what is true, what is just and what is loving, the result is inner peace and assurance and goodwill toward fellow human beings: this is cordising.

Truth, justice and charity are placed on the "I"Gram as **Routes of Cordising.**

Placement of ROC on "I"Gram

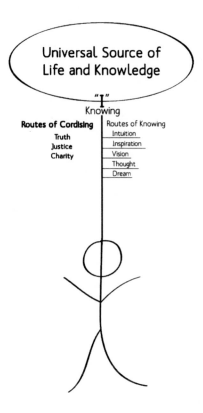

There is tremendous power in any one individual determining, willing, and taking action in light of that inner knowing. That action in turn affects everyone else as the opening scenes illustrate. In each of the scenes people either manifested cordising by observing actions of truth, justice and charity or they acted in a way that others were harmed. In one scene a German Nazi officer risked his own life by taking action that saved the life of a Jewish man, his ethnic enemy. In the other, a woman leaped from a bridge following shouts from frustrated drivers to do so.

Cordising – The Broad Picture in Human Relationships

What does it mean to be "in relationship" with another? Where do relationships start? Where do they end? What are valid expectations in a relationship? How does a person determine within self the boundaries of particular relationships?

The foundation and dynamics of all relationships are under the control of "I" moving in esca. The **Spirogram of Relationships** depicts self in relation to others, and can serve as a point of reference for examining the nature of various relationships. A relationship cannot exist unless there is some degree of caring even at the stranger level. The simple act of saying, "Excuse me" or holding a door for someone to enter requires a degree of caring.

**Spirogram of
Relationships**

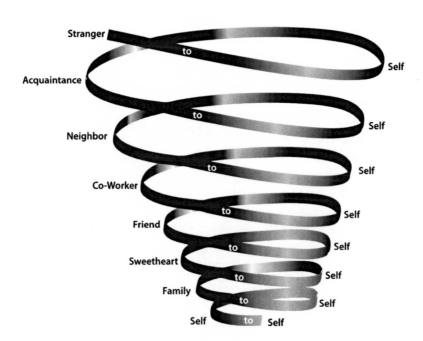

Every relationship depicted in the spirogram contains three important ingredients: trust, boundaries and expectations. The amount and kind of each ingredient varies according to the degree of intimacy. For example, trust is reliance on the integrity, strength and caring of another. It is clear that trust would be different at the stranger level than at the family level.

A boundary may be thought of as an imaginary line that defines ownership and responsibility between two people. Some boundaries are universal and are set by the nature and purpose of the relationship in society, such as in school, church and business. Other boundaries are unique and convey the limits that are set on the scope of intimacy or matters of a personal nature. Just as homeowners set physical property lines around their land, it is good for a person to set intellectual, physical and spiritual boundaries to help distinguish between what is one's responsibility and what is not. The boundaries that people set in relationships also indicate limits on how much of self is given and how much of another is received. Cordising helps to maintain boundaries within relationships. Each person in the relationship establishes, maintains and controls the boundary. Good judgment is required in each situation. One can say no without giving offense because the judgment is in regard to the actions, not the person. When one makes a judgment of "No, I will not help," it is not, "No, I will not help you," it is "No, I will not help in that process that you are asking of me." This kind of statement shows that the person exists apart from the other and is in control of self. The limits of giving and receiving will become apparent if one moves from the heart considering truth, justice and charity by responding to a "yes" or "no".

Valid expectations exist in every relationship. In a relationship with a stranger, there is the minimum expectation that no harm will be done. With an acquaintance it is valid to expect courtesy and acknowledgement, such as a good morning greeting. The relationship with a co-worker or classmate will involve working toward a common goal, and therefore cooperation can be expected. When a relationship is at the level of friend, sweetheart, family or spouse, it is essential to have a foundation that includes greater trust, loving, and greater giving along with forgiving. A solid foundation for more intimate relationships is laid over a period of time in a person's life, as one moves from blood relationships to other types of relationships.

The concept of cordising is much broader than the common idea of care in reference to one who is in need. Cordising encompasses the mutuality of asking for caring and of offering caring from the heart, caring *with* people rather than caring *for* people. If assisting or helping another person is part of a relationship, there is a request for care, accepted or refused, or an offer of care accepted or refused. In cordising, one may give or receive; each act is seen as equal and positive. In this way, the dignity of both the giver and the receiver is maintained, as responsibility and control of one's life remains in one's own hands. In cordising, no one moves in on another person, even with the best of intentions, without some indication that the person has asked for help. The concept of cordising is the bigger picture of what goes on in human relationships in society.

Cordising ~A Way of Life

Living a life characterized by actions based in cordising requires a lifelong pursuit and diligent self-control. It begins in the womb as the developing baby is desired, nourished and protected; in infancy as parents meet the needs for love through touch, sustenance, safety and shelter. It continues in childhood as parents set the example for children to be courteous, kind and respectful in word and action. In this environment of loving nurture the child can develop and sustain a focus on what is good, strong and positive in self and others. As children mature they can learn to exercise their will to resist taking actions that violate cordising. They learn to exercise their will to apologize and to ask forgiveness when their actions have hurt others. The formation of these habits provides the basis of moral excellence that can be sustained throughout life.

As we see our neighbors going through divorce with children caught in the middle; as we read in the newspaper that seven young men deliberately take the life of another because of romantic jealousy; when we see on the television national leaders caught in adultery and corporate executives jailed for corruption, we could feel hopeless and powerless. But the reality is that those who take action based in truth, justice and charity, who move with purpose and integrity, make a difference that is larger than the single act. There is hope for all persons when one person lives an honorable life; there is power for all persons when one person does the right thing. "The mind has exactly the same power as the hands; not merely to grasp the world, but to change it." [5]

"One ship drives east, and another west
With the self-same winds that blow;
'Tis the set of the sails
And not the gales, Which decides the way to go.
Like the winds of the sea are the ways of fate,
As we voyage along through life;
Tis the set of the soul that decides its goal,
And not the calm or the strife." [6]

---

[1] Script from the movie, *The Pianist;* A Roman Polanski Film, 2002.

[2] Reuters News (Seattle), "Egged on by Crowd, Woman Leaps from Seattle Bridge", August 28, 2001

[3] Seattle Times," Civic Soul Searching--Ugly Ship Canal Scene Prompts Grieving for City's Lost Civility", Editorial Page, August 31, 2001.

[4] Webster's New Collegiate Dictionary, op. cit.

[5] Wilson, Colin. English author. Motivational Quotes – Someday is Now Society. 2005. www.ericzorn.com/sin/quotes/

[6] Wilcox, Ella Wheeler, "Winds of Fate," Poems of Optimism, 2nd Edition. (London: Gay & Hancock. 1915).

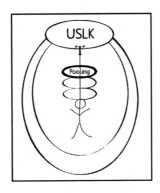

CHAPTER 7   THE POOLING PROCESS

"And then there is that knowing that I am everything I have been. All my thinking, feeling, doing, or saying in every moment of my life is integrated into the essence of me...registered, recorded,...like a giant pool...I can summon up memories, some hazy, some clear..." [1]

Three friends were reminiscing over lunch about their high school days. Their conversation moved from one topic to another: fellow students, teachers, football games they had attended, food in the cafeteria, clothing fads and favorite music. One person would start a topic with: "Do you remember?" Another person would elaborate, filling in with more detail.   It was astonishing how much they did remember and the way in which they were able to remember. They could picture their fellow students and teachers as they were then. They could say the words of football cheers and sing the high school song. They could smell the aromas of favorite and not so favorite cafeteria foods. Although the friends were sharing their memories with each other, each one had a different detail or perspective. They laughed over those memories of events and people during their high school days and they reflected upon the changes that had occurred since then. One person wondered aloud how they could have remembered all that "stuff". Herein is a fascinating story about a process in human beings that made that lunchtime conversation possible. The name of the process is pooling.

What is the pooling process?

In the pooling process the "I" of the human being is continuously depositing, blending, melding and interweaving present movings within the human being with the results of past movings within the human being. A moving may be thought of as the smallest unit of human action, visible and invisible, tangible and intangible, internal and external. The concept of the pooling process includes the notion of storage or a storehouse for all that human beings experience in living life. Each and every moving in the human being has at least one result or effect and these are stored in the pooling process. For example, the three friends reminiscing over lunch about their high school days will store the results of that experience in their respective pooling processes. Each of the friends will store something slightly different from the other two, reflecting the feature of the uniqueness of every human being. Yet all three friends will store something about that lunchtime conversation, underscoring the fact that the pooling process is present in every human being as part of the human "blueprint".

The pooling process enables human beings to build on experiences of the past, to understand present movings and to plan future movings in self. The process of pooling also makes deliberating, recalling, remembering, learning, planning, deciding, judging and a host of other human activities possible. Thus, nothing of a person ever is lost. Human beings are, in every moment of living, the result of what they have been. To extend this idea a little further, consider the fact that any change a person makes in the present sets the stage for different results in the future. For example, a student who plans to spend fifteen additional minutes per school day studying French is setting the stage for increased fluency in the language and perhaps a better

76

score on the final examination if the plan is carried out. The improved understanding of French that results from additional study is stored in the pooling process. Similarly, a basketball player planning to practice at least ten free throw shots per day is setting the stage for increased skill in shooting free throw shots if the plan is carried out. The results of the player's practice are stored in his or her pooling process to be retrieved during the game.

These examples illustrate something else about the pooling process: the frequency with which other processes are involved and necessary in order to make beneficial use of what is stored. For example, both the student of French and the basketball player intend certain actions and engage their wills to carry out those actions. Each implements a plan and at the appointed time, the "I" of each of the two persons, moving in their respective pooling processes, retrieves the results of their study and practice to achieve the desired ends. The processes of intending, willing, planning and implementing are going on simultaneously. It is not possible for someone else to know why each of the two persons is engaging in those actions unless each one tells us. Only the person taking the action knows for certain why he or she is doing so in light of the personal and individual meaning that the action has at that moment in time.

The pooling process also makes it possible for human beings to look at the past from different angles and for different purposes. Even unpleasant or painful experiences can contribute in a positive way to a person's life. A person may retrieve an experience from the distant past and look at it from a more recent and beneficial perspective. For example, a child may have an unpleasant experience of being disciplined by a parent for telling a lie. When the child becomes an adult, he or she may remember the unpleasant experience but now may look at it from the perspective of having learned the importance of being truthful. When the same adult becomes a parent, he or she may recall that experience from the distant past and consider it from a present understanding of the importance of being truthful. The parent may then take action in light of parental knowing of this child at this moment and the responsibility of every parent to teach and model the ways of truthful living. It may be helpful to picture the original experience as a mirrored ballroom globe that reflects thousands of different points of light as it turns. It is the privilege and responsibility of each person in living life to turn the globe around so as to obtain maximum benefit from the light that it disperses.

What does the pooling process look like and how does it work?

Some parts of the pooling process are well organized. For example, most people can recite a poem, say a prayer or sing a favorite song from the past, just as the three friends did at lunch. This example also illustrates that the "I" of the human being is able to engage deliberately in the pooling process in order to retrieve a memory stored there. Other parts of the pooling process are not as well organized. For example, most people engage for varying lengths of time in non-deliberate, non-specific excursions through past experiences in a general way, viewing, reviewing and combining actual experiences and possible experiences. This may be one of the features of what is commonly called day dreaming.

If it were possible to look at a cross section of one person's pooling process, an outside observer would see myriad movings in no explainable order. There might be shelves or layers or compartments containing an assortment or aggregate of movings. But an outside observer would not be able to explain the way in which those movings are arranged or ordered. The specific order, arrangement and boundary of material in the pooling process are part of the uniqueness of every human being.

Another characteristic of movings in the pooling process results in the formation of whole experiences that enable a person to say, for example: "I have extensive experience in (topic: teaching, business, art, driving, writing)". This is made possible by a process of attraction and attachment that occurs between movings. It is likely that movings carry an electromagnetic charge or code as they enter the pooling process. Coding or charge affects

78

the destination and distribution of movings and influences how they combine with other movings to form an aggregate of experience. Throughout their journey in the pooling process, movings are influenced by the "I" knowing of the person, moving in all the other processes simultaneously. This is the way in which the "I" of the human being shapes memory and experience.

Pooling process and everyday living

There are many sayings in everyday life that speak to the importance and benefits of experience to human beings: Experience is the best teacher. Listen to the voice of experience. What we choose to forget, we are sure to repeat.

Each person's pooling process may be thought of as a personal treasure chest, filled with those thoughts, wishes, hopes and dreams, feelings and actions, and all the things that make each person the unique being that he or she is. This is how wisdom grows and how the bonds of family history are passed from generation to generation. The pooling process makes life for human beings both rich and real. This is what made the high school reminiscences between those three friends possible and fascinating.

---

[1] Kinlein, M. Lucille. What am I doing with Who I Am? (Minneapolis, MN, National Center of Kinlein, 1995), p. 55.

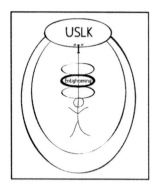

CHAPTER 8   ENLIGHTENING PROCESS

"Earlier in the day we had had a tussle over the words 'm-u-g' and 'w-a-t-e-r'. Miss Sullivan had tried to impress upon me that 'm-u-g' is mug *and 'w-a-t-e-r' is* water ...

We walked down the path to the well-house. . . Someone was drawing water and my teacher placed my hand under the spout. As the cool stream rushed over one hand, she spelled into the other the word water, *first slowly, then rapidly. I stood still , my whole attention focused upon the motions of her fingers. Suddenly I felt a misty consciousness as of something forgotten -- a thrill of returning thought; and somehow the mystery of language was revealed to me. I knew then that "w-a-t-e-r" meant the wonderful cool something that was flowing over my hand. That living word awakened my soul, gave it light, hope, joy, set it free!"* Helen Keller [1]

The obvious is often right before a person's eyes; yet it is not seen. Experiences can show a person different aspects of a small truth or a big truth, but the whole is not "seen" or the significance of it is not grasped. Time passes, then -- "Eureka!" it is seen. The light goes on, but it is an internal light, produced by a process within the person. The person engages in a process called *enlightening.* Light is shed on something, making it more clear. All that has preceded this sudden (or gradual) "seeing" becomes a complete and sometimes breathtaking picture. A concept is grasped. It is through this enlightening process in the human being that an understanding is illuminated.

The stimulus for the enlightening process can come from any of the processes in self animate or it can be triggered by events external to the person. It can be in regard to any aspect of living, past or present. There is a joining of pieces that culminates in *enlightenment* through the *enlightening process.* It includes a sense of understanding significance and influence in regard to some aspect of living life. First, there is a working through all the processes in self animate, then the enlightening occurs on a shaft of information, or a comment, or an idea. A spotlight may be shone on a tiny piece of the big jigsaw puzzle of living life or a larger area may be spotlighted. It can be the equivalent of an explosion of light or the gradual illumination of slowly turning up the rheostat on a dimmer switch.

The enlightening process has an ephemeral, ethereal quality in that the light it sheds is so illuminating that it can't be put into words. This quality differentiates enlightening from intuition in that the latter is more narrow, more contained--a shaft of knowing something that is direct in regard to a particular incident or movement. Enlightenment can sometimes follow closely on the heels of the intuitionary process. The enlightening process has been said to have "lit the way" for an important decision or action taken.

Just as one cannot be empowered by another, a person cannot be enlightened by someone else. The enlightening process occurs within the person moving in esca, as that person sees with more clarity an aspect or pieces of the whole coming together. The process of enlightening cannot be put into words, but the trigger for this process can sometimes be identified and the results may be expressed in words or phrases such as, "Yes..I see..." or "Aha!" or "In light of this that I now see, my direction is more clear."

As in all the movings in self animate-corporeal, one's enlightening can be built on or it can be ignored. It can be recognized when it occurs and appropriate action taken, or it can be pushed back down for various reasons. For example, the person may attempt to justify thoughts or actions and say to self, "It doesn't matter what I saw," and "I will not look at the significance of what I am seeing." Or the enlightenment can provide a new frame of reference and impetus for learning, understanding, and further enlightening.

The "I" was conceived with knowing; yet it takes the living of life for a person to come to understand that knowing. As life is lived, more knowledge is gained through many different experiences. The human being uses the tools of intuition, inspiration, vision, thought and dream in the acquiring of this knowledge. Pieces of a whole are grasped and understood. In other processes the person works with what these pieces mean, weighs them in light of Truth, Justice and Charity, and blends them with past experiences. Through the enlightening process the person sees the whole, grasps the significance and an understanding is illuminated. If "I" wills to build on what was illuminated, life's journey can become richer and richer as the "I" comes to see both what was known from conception and the jewels of Truth revealed as life is lived.

"I left the well-house eager to learn. Everything had a name, and each name gave birth to a new thought. As we returned to the house every object which I touched seemed to quiver with life. That was because I saw everything with the strange, new sight that had come to me. ...
It would have been difficult to find a happier child than I was as I lay in my crib at the close of that eventful day and lived over the joys it had brought me, and for the first time longed for a new day to come."[2]

---

[1] Keller, H. <u>The Story of My Life</u>. 1902. (New York, Penguin, 1988), p 17-18
[2] Keller, H. IBID. p 18

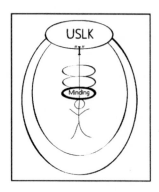

CHAPTER 9   THE MINDING PROCESS

"How can you get very far
If you don't know Who You Are?
How can you do what you ought,
If you don't know What You've Got?
And if you don't know which to do
Of all the things in front of you,
Then what you'll have when you get through
Is just a mess without a clue
Of all the best that can come true,
If you know What and Which and Who." [1]

Pooh says it all. In the richness and complexities of everyday living, there is a logical necessity for a process that results in an ordering of all the details in order to permit a visible, concrete, coherent manifestation of all the movings in self animate. How is this ordering of details, sorting through of options and organizing of actions accomplished? How does some of the splendor of the movings in the invisible, intangible, abstract aspect of self animate get translated or formulated into words and actions manifested in self corporeal? How do human beings bring an embryonic vision to concrete reality? How does the will find a way? Some answers to these questions can be found in the process of minding.

In the minding process, the person selects content from the pooling process, sorts and organizes it, and formulates it into words and actions. The movings in this process are going on all the time, but the activity is most concentrated just before a person takes overt action by speaking, writing, signing and by moving the body. Compared to other processes in self animate, the minding process is the least abstract. It's action has been likened to a factory. Materials come into a factory and equipment is used to make a product. Materials for the minding process come from all the other processes in self animate via the pooling process. The equipment in the minding process is language and the product is words. Once the human being has developed language, including vocabulary, rules of grammar and syntax, the equipment is fully operational. Then, the verbal factory within the minding process begins the selection of words to convey the speaker's meaning. The process may appear to be automatic and instantaneous until the person slows down to find the correct word; as, for example when someone exclaims: "I know what I want to say; I just can't find the words!"

Another phase in the operations of the minding process involves ordering and sequencing. The minding process is engaged to organize the features of a decision made in the pooling process. The sequence of actions necessary to carry out the decision, the choice of optional paths and the timing of actions are organized in the minding process. It is here where a person works with the factors of time, place and physical laws as possibilities are considered and the carrying out of actions is designed.

On the "I" Gram, the minding process is depicted as an ellipse closest to the figure representing the physical body of the human being. This placement indicates that the minding process is closest to the concrete, visible action phase of human endeavor.

The Person in the Minding Process

The starting point for tracking the invisible movings that reach the minding process would be the continuous flow of material entering the pooling process from all the other processes in self animate. This forms the raw material for more discrete actions within the minding process as the person distills and organizes the results of those movings into the possibility of concrete words and actions.

The results of the minding process go through the brain template into the cells of the body and may take the form of words, gestures, facial expressions, and other overt actions. The trigger for those actions may come from routes of cordising, routes of knowing, or any of the other processes in self animate. Whatever the source, the words and actions a person selects in the minding process convey the results of movings in the other processes.

Two specific processes in self animate are inextricably interwoven: a willingness to convey the results of the process and a significance, purpose or meaning of what is conveyed by the words or actions. The minding process is universal to all human beings but the ways of moving are unique in each one. To the degree that words contain evidence of those intangible movings in self animate, they contain the very self of the speaker and affirm the individuality and indivisibility of that person.

Words and Actions in the Minding Process

It is inherent in human beings to be rational and to convey meaning through an orderly structure in an orderly manner. Words are the most accurate and precise way for a person to convey meaning because their definitions provide an objective frame of reference both for the speaker and for the listener. Even with words, meaning is never conveyed completely because the fullness of it resides in the person, not in the words themselves. Words may be thought of as clothing on the speaker's meaning and the clothing may not be a perfect fit.

Gestures and expressions formed in the minding process also convey meaning but not as accurately or precisely as words because actions depend upon context for their interpretation. For example, picture a person with arms flailing in the air. What does that mean? In one context, it might convey that the person is exasperated. In another context, the flailing might convey a person struggling to prevent a fall. In still another context, it might convey humor or comedy. In other words, gestures and expressions are interpreted by the observer according to the context in which they occur. The possibilities for misunderstandings and errors are greatly increased when the people involved have not agreed on the context.

The Minding Process in Everyday Living

Since both speaking and listening are daily activities that involve moving in the minding process, there is much that speakers can do to enhance the clarity of what is said and heard. For example, the more words a person has learned to use in light of their root definitions, the easier it will be for the person to select those words that best convey the intended meaning. The more precisely the speaker selects and arranges those words, the more precisely meaning can be conveyed. Ignoring the rules of grammar and syntax may leave the listener perplexed. Anyone who has ever learned another language probably can relate a hilarious or embarrassing anecdote that resulted from being a novice at grammar and syntax in the new language. The more aware the speaker is of the purpose, significance or intention for speaking, the easier it is to organize and sequence the points in the minding process so as to convey meaning. The listener's job is to receive the words completely as they are given before working with them or responding to them. It is not helpful for the listener to be searching for words to form a response while receiving the speaker's words. Listening without interruption keeps the words clean and clear of interpretation. It also honors the unique quality of the speaker's meaning without placing one's own meaning over it. Finally, listening in this way conveys respect for the dignity of the person speaking.[1]

Ordinary living requires a person to stay focused and organized much of the time or be labeled the classic absent-minded professor. Without balance, it is possible for a person to stay so busy lining up the details of planning and organizing actions in the minding process, that the more abstract processes of reflecting, thinking through, and integrating potential action with values held, are cut short. The result can be impulsive or shallow behavior of limited value to self and others. One way to achieve balance is to consider the effects of words spoken and actions taken. If benefits to self and others are not apparent, it may be helpful to look more closely at what preceded those words and actions. In general, the more the person wills to seek truth, justice and charity and to act in light of them, the more benefit can be expected. As the person finds balance by being firmly anchored in the "why" of an action, the "how" is more easily designed in the minding process.

Many grand accomplishments of the past were brought about by individuals finding ways to bring something to fruition, day by day, step by step. In the same way, many small wonders happen every day. What great thoughts are yet to be worded? What unique visions, grounded in truth, are still to be manifested by human beings....If we just have *"a clue of all the best that can come true, If we know What and Which and Who..."* and if we know why.

---

[1] Kinlein, M. Lucille et al. <u>The Joy of Listening,</u> Minneapolis, MN, National Center of Kinlein, 1993), p. 62-64

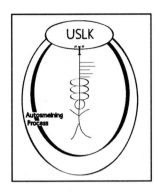

CHAPTER 10   AUTOSMEINENING PROCESS

"There is nothing in the world, I venture to say, that would so effectively help one to survive the worst conditions, as the knowledge that there is meaning in one's life." Viktor Frankl [1]

Since the beginning of time, human beings have pondered these questions: what is the meaning of life, of living and of death? Interwoven with this quest to understand the universal meaning of life is the quest of each individual to come to understand more about "Why am I here? What is the meaning of my life?" These questions and ones like them are in the very fabric of human beings in their search for meaning.

Where does meaning come from? Do human beings invent meaning or do they detect it? Is it inside of them, outside of them, or both? Why is meaning so important to human beings, so important in fact, that if Frankl is right, their very lives depend upon it?

Meaning is defined as **"The end, purpose or significance of something."** [2]   The breadth of the concept of meaning can be more fully understood by looking at its characteristics:

1. **It is intangible and abstract,** that is, the meaning of

something cannot be grasped by the senses alone. For example, a person can touch and taste an apple, but the significance of that experience is abstract: perhaps the person takes it as a sign of hope; perhaps it's meaning is rooted in childhood memories.

2. **Meaning is universal.** For example, all living beings have a purpose that is common to all living beings. The birth, life and death of human beings have a purpose and significance that is common to all humans. The ability of plants to synthesize chlorophyll from sunlight has universal significance. The ability of electrons to bond elements together is a universal purpose of electrons.

3. Paradoxically, **meaning is unique**. For example, the significance of hydrogen atoms bonding with oxygen to form water in this drop of rain, falling on this corn plant, at this moment in the drought in Iowa is unique. The purpose and significance of one person's life is unique, as is each moment of that individual's life. If the metaphor of a large mosaic is used to represent the big picture of life, it shows that each person has a place assigned to put that unique tile. If someone does not fill in a particular space, it will take many people working longer and harder to fill it in.[3] The meaning of any one person's life is irreplaceable and unrepeatable.

4. Efforts made to grasp the intangible, universal, unique meaning of an experience or an aspect of life reveals many dimensions. For these reasons, **meaning is larger than words and can never be conveyed <u>fully</u> through language.**

The complexity of meaning is apparent in these characteristics. This concept "is multifaceted because all human beings live life according to the meaning they adopt, integrate, understand, incorporate, name or search for." [4]

Whenever a human being asks, "Why?" a search for meaning has begun. Using logic and reason, the tools of philosophy, a person can begin to answer "Why?" Why do atoms have electrons? Why does a caterpillar spin its cocoon when it does? Why do plants produce chlorophyll? Why do human beings question? The use of reason can lead to the conclusion that there must be purpose in a world of such complex order, because order flows from purpose. Philosophy investigates the nature of this order and the why of it.

What is the <u>ultimate</u> end, purpose or significance of electrons, cocoons, chlorophyll, human rationality, or one person's life? The total meaning of ALL THAT IS is beyond the ability of the human being to grasp through reason alone. The search for the meaning of life leads one right to the bridge between philosophy and theology. In order to answer the question, the question of the ultimate Why, one must turn to the realm of belief, faith and revelation addressed by theology. The theory of moving in esca does not address theology, but speaks from a philosophical view that provides sound footing for looking at how human beings relate to meaning.

Throughout time, different philosophical views of meaning have been developed; some of them still evident in society today, provide slippery footing and have many pitfalls. For example, one view is that meaning is found only in self. There is no universal or absolute meaning to life. I alone invent the meaning of my life. Another view is that meaning is found only in the world or in the Universal Source of Life and Knowledge. I have no way to access or comprehend the meaning of Life or of my life. A third view is that there is no meaning to life.

The <u>above</u> views demonstrate a **<u>departure</u> <u>from</u>** the theory of moving in esca which, in contrast, is based on these premises:
1. There is an absolute or universal meaning to life.
2. Each person knows something about the meaning of my life, unique, and Life, universal.
3. There is a way to access and comprehend something of the meaning of my life, unique, and Life, universal.

Autosmeinen

Since meaning is abstract, greater than words, universal and unique how can human beings access and understand something of the meaning in life? The concept in the theory of moving in esca that explains how human beings work with meaning is called **autosmeinen.** The word *autosmeinen* is derived from the Greek word, *autos*: self and Old Dutch, *meinen*: meaning. Literally then, autosmeinen is self meaning.

Autosmeinen is a part of the intangible, invisible aspect of "I" Knowing - the self animate. In the theory of moving in esca, each person has received "I" Knowing with the breath of life from the very moment of conception. Universally contained in the "I" Knowing of each human being is a knowing of something about the meaning of life and death, and something of the unique purpose of one's own life and death.

Consider the implications of the previous paragraph. If true, this knowing helps a person make choices about what paths to pursue, even though the light shone by the knowing is dim. It helps a person gain understanding about paths not taken or already taken. If human beings are conceived as "empty slates," then why cannot parents mold their sons and daughters so as to make the parents' dreams come true? History is replete with stories written about individuals having a sense of a unique calling or destiny to fulfill; and they seek to do so often despite what anyone wanted for them.

Although humans are conceived with knowing, it is obvious that they do not know everything. Each person has a unique part of the whole meaning of it all. This part or piece that that individual person has been given is called the **triangle of meaning**. It is designated as a Triangle to indicate that each person has a precise small part of an intricate, orderly grand design.

What is in this triangle of meaning? The size, the degree, the depth and breadth of the meaning is unique, yet every person's triangle contains these basics: .

1. Life comes from a source outside all life forms.

2. Human life has a quality that other forms of life do not have.

3. Everything from the Universal Source of Life and Knowledge has purpose.

4. Every human being has been given that which is needed to understand the purpose of life.

5. Each person is responsible for the unique piece of meaning given to him or her.

In the process of **autosmeinening,** the person references moment to moment living in light of one's unique triangle of meaning. In the "I" Gram autosmeinen is drawn as a large ellipse surrounding all the other processes, except phases of consciousness.

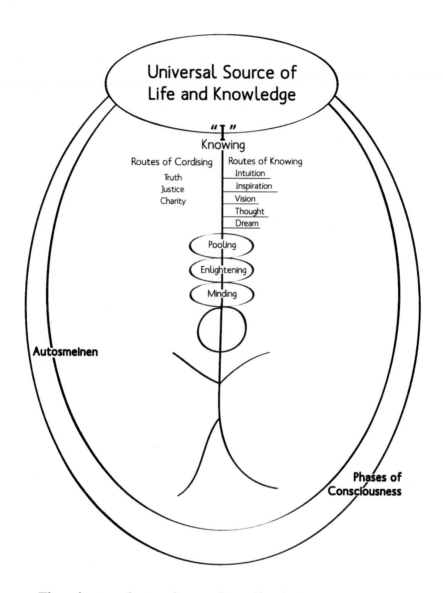

The picture above shows that all of the processes of self animate-corporeal are referenced in light of autosmeining. All actions of a human being occur within that ellipse of autosmeinen. Through phases of consciousness, the outermost ellipse, the "I" controls what action is taken in light of the meaning to self.

If "meaning is in each human being and is unique in each

human being, logically there has to be a Source from which this meaning flows. If there are parts of meaning that each human has, then somewhere there has to be all meaning. The concept of All Meaning is termed **omnimeinen** ..." [5] The origin of autosmeinen is omnimeinen and omnimeinen is an attribute of the Universal Source of Life and Knowledge. The triangle of meaning connects each person to omnimeinen.

Autosmeinen and phases of consciousness are the two factors that significantly distinguish human beings from other life forms. Only a human being can ask what is the meaning of life. Only a human being has the will power to act or not to act in light of the answers found. It is the privilege and responsibility of all human beings to examine self in light of all meaning. The reality of will power allows human beings to act in light of what was seen during such self-examination.

The **autosmeinening process** is defined as the referencing of moment-to-moment living in light of the meaning one holds. It is the wordless process by which the person evaluates the results of all the movings in self animate. The autosmeinening process is a continuous moving in the human being from the moment of conception onward throughout life to death. In this process the person follows truth that is outside all human beings[6] and relates the bigness of that truth to the meaning of "my" life. This is truly moving in one's uniqueness. There is no other human being who ever lived, is living or will live that will ever be a duplicate of me, of you, of anyone else.

In the autosmeinening process in daily life, the actions a person takes may produce either expansion or contraction in the triangle of meaning. "The autosmeinening process in a person is the moment of being in touch or willing not to be in touch with truth, justice and charity which takes the person closest to the Universal Source of Life and Knowledge. That is the fullness of autosmeinening. As the person lines up "my" meaning with the all meaning contained in the Universal Source of Life and Knowledge, the "I" of the person moves from the limits and bounds of everyday living to the boundlessness inherent in the first cause, uncaused, the U.S.L.K.   Autosmeinening, therefore, is infinite in terms of significance, while the other processes are finite in terms of significance." [7]

The autosmeinening process is the most integrative process of a person. It is the process that best accounts for the uniqueness of every human being. Through this process the "I" of the person brings together what was worked with through intuition, inspiration, vision, thought and dream; what was weighed in light of truth, justice and charity; the results of pooling, enlightening and minding; sensations registered and known, and results of physiologizing.   Through all of these processes the person apprehends meaning and wills how to act in light of it. The ripple effect of each choice made is wide, because each person's triangle of meaning has touch points with those of others.

What an inspiration it is to see one person find the courage and strength to fulfill his or her purpose using individual talents in a unique way. For that person and for each of us, recognition of the contribution that each of us has to make that no one else can make, provides both solid footing and the impetus to face the challenge of filling in our tiles in the mosaic of life.

---

[1] Frankl, Viktor, Man's Search for Meaning, 1964, p. 164
[2] Random House Dictionary of the English Language, op.cit.
[3] Kinlein, M. Lucille, Moving That Power Within, op. cit., p. 48
[4] Kinlein, M. Lucille, James, Annette, Martin, Rita Joy of listening, op. cit., p. 19
[5] IBID, p.19
[6] Kinlein, M. Lucille, Consultation III with Karen Carpenter, August 12, 1998, p.3
[7] IBID

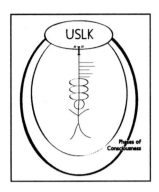

CHAPTER 11   PHASES OF CONSCIOUSNESS

"The human will, that force unseen,

The offspring of a deathless Soul,

Can hew the way to any goal,

Though walls of granite intervene."[1]

Red-faced, slippery, and wailing, the newborn human enters into the light of day whole and complete. This whole little human is made up of parts. The part called self corporeal can be seen. The part called self animate cannot be seen. The seen and the unseen, both parts of the whole human being, function by means of processes. The human being, child or adult, is a dynamic organism, physical, rational, and spiritual, in nature. This organism is functional, orderly, and purposeful. Function is the offspring of the physical nature, order is the offspring of the rational nature, and purpose is the offspring of the spiritual nature. The many movings within the person would effect no purposeful end were they not controlled.

In the theory of moving in esca it is the "I" of the person that is the ultimate source of control of "my Self". All of the processes in self animate and self corporeal are controlled by "I". All of the wondering, deciding, contemplating, analyzing and choosing a person engages in every day; all of the digesting, absorbing, assimilating, and excreting that goes on, all of the feelings, are under the control of "I". It is the "I" of the person that holds the power over any action taken, from the most overt to the most concealed, the most important to the most trivial, the most intended to the most automatic. This factor of control bespeaks the responsibility of every human being to be care-full of the next word spoken, the next thought formed, the next act undertaken. This is the great power of, "Yes, I will", or "No, I will not".

The process which underlies the control is the person, moving in the **phases of consciousness.** Phases of consciousness are those states of awareness in every person in terms of willing and intending actions and results of actions, paying attention to the action in order to ensure the desired result, and finally, the initiation of the action which is to be taken immediately. Any action a person takes proceeds from the impetus of it to the final result via moving in the phases of consciousness.

The phases of consciousness are named volitional, intentional, attentional, and overt actional. They are called phases because they can be distinguished as parts in the process which precede all other actions of living. Since there is never a time a person is not in action on some level, every human being is in each one of the phases of consciousness in varying degrees of intensity, at every moment of living. A person can focus awareness to a greater or lesser degree in any one of the phases at a particular point in time. The phases of consciousness depict the process of control that every person has in regard to every action taken in living life.

The **Volitional** phase of consciousness is that state of the person in any degree of awareness of unequivocal willing of a thought, word, or deed in either their results or consequences. Volition is the deepest, most internal act of reflection, concentration, and deliberation, stemming from a set of values, with the willing of an action being the characteristic of this phase of consciousness. The results the of willing of an act are worthy of weighty consideration and contemplation. It is clear that there is a difference between the firmness of being willing to enter a new life state, such as marriage, and the casualness of selecting one food item over another at the deli. The volitional phase involves deliberation and concentration. It is unknowable by others unless voiced by the person: "I will to think, feel, say, do."

The **Intentional** phase of consciousness is that state of the person in any degree of awareness, intending an effect of word or action. Intentional is the phase in which motivations, purposes, and desires, stemming from a set of values, precede action or occur during the action itself. There is a difference between the firmness of intention to persevere in getting an education and the casualness of intention to pick up a grocery item on the way home. This phase involves deliberation and concentration. It is unknowable by others unless voiced by the person: "I intend by this decision...", "My motive is..."

The **Attentional** phase of consciousness is the state of awareness in the person of the immediate focus of attention; the state in which the person is most aware of what is being spoken or thought or action taken. This phase involves less deliberation and varying degrees of concentration. It is unknowable by others unless voiced by the person: "As I was driving to work, I was thinking about the figures for the report that is due this afternoon."

Overt Actional is the phase which most immediately precedes overt, visible physical actions. It is the final surveillance of self before omission or commission of an action. This phase involves the least deliberation and varying degrees of concentration. It is important to note, that although another can see the overt action, the meaning of the action cannot be known unless voiced by the person.

Moving in phases of consciousness yields great consequences in terms of impact in living life. This is where one determines, I **will** take this action; I **will not** take that action. All actions in self corporeal result from movings in self animate through the phases of consciousness. There is no action taken by a person that does not have the permission of the will.

Because no man is an island, any action taken by any one individual affects the lives of all other individuals. Such effect may be direct or indirect. This entwining of human lives has been a point of comfort as well as sorrow since the dawn of time.

Self-control, accountability, and responsibility, the result of moving in the processes in self animate and self corporeal, are at the heart of a civilized society. Every act has a consequence, every consequence has meaning. As the wailing newborn develops physically, he or she also develops intellectually and spiritually. Initially, the child's priority is solely What I want. As life teaches its lessons, the child learns to weigh What I want against What happens if I get what I want. At this point, consequences take on meaning for that young person. Meaning influences and directs human actions; will controls human actions. At the foundation of meaning is the concept of right and wrong. Not everything that is 'right' is pleasurable and not everything that is 'wrong' is painful. Since pleasure tends to bias human judgment, one must, by an act of will, prepare for personal sacrifice if one is desiring to look to the good of others. This may, perhaps, be the ultimate control of self and is, indeed, the power of, "Yes, I will", or "No, I will not".

"It is not enough to know right and to know wrong, we must habituate ourselves to take pleasure in doing good things and be pained by doing bad things." (Aristotle)

---

[1] Wilcox, Ella Wheeler. *"Will"*, _Poems of Power._ (Chicago: W.B. Conkey Company, 1901), p. 116,

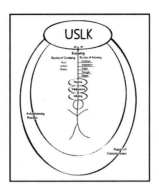

CHAPTER 12   WHO AM I AND WHY AM I HERE?

"All the evidence available in the biological sciences supports the core proposition...that the cosmos is a specially designed whole with life and mankind as its fundamental goal and purpose, a whole in which all facets of reality have their meaning and explanation in this central fact."[1]

This book began with a mystery exploring the nature of being human, describing universal processes within every person. And now it ends with a mystery: Who am I and Why am I Here? The theory of moving in esca anchors these questions in the truth that every human being is conceived in a state of knowing and has been given the tools necessary to gain an understanding of that knowing as life unfolds. Every threshold of understanding reached opens new vistas to explore. No human being can ever see the full picture of life and how intricately one person's life is interwoven into that whole. Because of this fact, every human being will always be able to reach for more understanding of the mystery.

From the mystery inherent in the conception of a human being who carries a piece of the past yet is a totally new person, to the mystery of the last breath, one inescapably leaves some mark of his or her unique existence. In the transition from conception to birth of the newborn and beyond, the development of each person unfolds according to a unique genetic coding. The most observable growth during infancy is physical development with its wide variation in patterns of weight, length/height and coordination of body movements such as sitting, standing and running. Movings in self animate, though also unique, are less obvious in the infant because of the absence of understandable language. Until language is developed, the abstract, internal movings in self animate can never be known by others unless the person voices them, but are nonetheless stirring and unfolding. Awareness, thinking, and self-control are examples of invisible, intangible aspects of being human, unknown to others without the words of the speaker. These movings in self animate-corporeal contain the first glimpses one sees of the infant's sense of Who am I.

The development of language in the growing child is a significant milestone. The selection and arrangement of words enable the youngster to convey a portion of his or her meaning and the child begins to grasp the significance and power of words. This is readily evident when one hears a two-year-old proclaim, "NO!". The responses of adults to the words of the child are important influences in the further development of that child's sense of Who am I. Expressions of affection and encouragement and firm guidance all contribute to the development of trust in an infant and youngster. That trust, in turn, sets the foundation for the many relationships with fellow human beings that will develop across the decades of life: friendships at school, romantic attractions in adolescence, employer-employee commitment, marriage, community/national citizenship.

As a child grows and explores self and the environs of society, there is increasing awareness of the control he or she has in living life. This process is aided and guided by adults in the child's life, first by the parents, then by the extended family, then at school. Although the child of this age will not ask the questions, Who am I or Why am I here, the answers to those questions at this time are shaped by adults as they introduce the idea of responsibility to self and others. The following excerpt from the journal of a student teacher describes how one adult is aiding and guiding a first grader through the process of accepting responsibility for her behavior:

"Our school has an Assertive Discipline Program...They schedule a reward for each month. Any student who received a lunch detention or worse during that month cannot participate.... The students got to make their own sundaes after lunch. However, both Dillon and Noah were unable to participate. Noah took it in stride and understood why he couldn't participate. Dillon, on the other hand, became quite emotional and began saying, "Everyone hates me. I can never do anything right." ...I sat with her and tried to change some of those statements to a more accurate representation of what this all really meant. Simply, that she didn't follow the rules and received a detention ...and therefore couldn't have the reward today. She is having a very difficult time right now with her behavior, emotions, and social skills. I think it's important that she be made responsible for her actions and made to follow the rules, but it is equally important to make sure that she receives support to help her do this and to keep her from feeling bad about herself. It's a hard balance to maintain... On one hand, I feel very sorry for her...yet I feel I have a responsibility to help her by teaching her to follow the rules and manage her behavior...Setting small goals over time would really be helpful for her and the consistency would also serve her well." [2]

The guidance and concern that this adult provided has the potential for being pivotal in the development of a healthy sense of responsibility in that child.

During the years of adolescence and early adulthood, new questions may arise: What is the meaning of my life and my place in the world? At this stage the answers to these questions are very much influenced by choices made by the person, choices that can be strongly affected by the opinions of peers.

Moving into adulthood, a person gains maturity and a perspective of self that is steadier. With that steadier perspective comes a broader understanding that the freedom to grow is accompanied by responsibilities for self and to others. As one exercises free will and the power to choose, the results of those choices can bring benefit or harm. The consequences of the choices made are the sole responsibility of the person who has made them. However, at any point in living life day to day, one can make another choice based on new data or simply because of a change of heart. For example, a person can choose to leave an unpleasant or dissatisfying career or marriage or decide to resolve the situation with a shift in thought or attitude.

Every individual faces challenges and crises in living life. Some persons are born with or develop physical or mental conditions that result from damage to processes in the cells, tissues and organs. Some individuals experience tragic losses or betrayals that are coded and stored within. Others suffer injury through the intentional or unintentional actions of others. Yet the "I" of each of those persons, moving in esca, remains undamaged, whole, perfect, and free. Thus human beings are able to face challenges by building on a steady point that is good, strong, and beautiful. It is this perspective of "I" that becomes the bulwark in facing the challenges of living life and helps human beings to achieve the unique purposes of their lives.

As men and women approach mid-life, they begin a review of their accomplishments and aspirations. Answering the questions, Who am I and Why am I here often take on greater significance or urgency. This retrospection is analogous to a hiker climbing a mountain with overlooks at various plateaus. The plateaus enable the climber to rest, to absorb the larger view, and to assess whether or not the selected pathway is the best route to the top. During this time, some persons institute a mid-course correction by moving in a different direction. The new direction may be in regard to career, relationships, education, allocations of time and resources or some other aspect of life. The uniqueness of one's moving in the invisible processes in self-animate enables the person at this age to act in light of this retrospection.

During the senior years, family and faith often take on greater significance. The wisdom that has accrued, trials and tribulations endured, and the legacy of contributions to humanity, may bring to a person a sense of contentment about a life well lived, about a plan brought to fruition. With increasing awareness of the passing of time, a person may grow in the appreciation of each moment in its freshness as it dances like a snowflake, unique, unspoiled and unrepeatable. On the other hand, a person may have a sense of remorse or regret or guilt in not having experienced opportunities more fully or deeply or may even feel bitter about the circumstances of his or her life. Often there is greater awareness of the inner knowing and appreciation of the Universal Source of Life and Knowledge. This knowing may become more vibrant, radiant and evident within the person during the later decades of life or may become only vaguely remembered as death approaches.

It has been said that the unexamined life is not worth living. Introspective practices enable a person to get the most from past experiences and to navigate future events or transitions with greater peace of mind; confidence; acceptance; with fewer regrets and more wisdom. A person may come to understand and appreciate that life has a rhythm, an ebb and flow. Through these reflective periods over a lifetime, a person may move from being knowledgeable to becoming wise. One learns how to recognize what matters and why. In looking at self one might ask:

1. What have been the highlights and disappointments of my journey in life? Do any amends need to be made that might help diminish regrets?

2. How have my intentions to honor the values of truth, justice and charity been manifested?
3. To what degree have the choices I've made been in alignment with my understanding of the Universal Source of Life and Knowledge?
4. Is a mid-course correction whispering to me? Is there a person who might be able to assist me in gaining clarity as to how I want to continue in my journey?

And so, this book ends but the mystery continues: What is the significance of being human, or, WHY am I here? The theory of moving in esca provides an anchor in the ongoing search for that understanding. Since the actions of any one person have an effect on the whole of humankind, coming to know one's own purpose gives rise to actions which have an effect on oneself, one's family and one's community. Whatever you may think about yourself and however long you may have thought it, you are intricately connected to all of creation, you are not alone; yet you alone, in essence, hold the keys to liberate the future. [3] You know yourself better than anyone else can know you; you are in control of the actions you take and are responsible for the consequences; you are human, hence you have dignity; you have the power within yourself to take actions in living your life, moment to moment. The significance of any one human being is beyond apprehension on a material level. Therefore, that knowledge behooves one to live one's life carefully yet with a willingness to risk it all for the sake of honor, integrity and holding to that which is true, that which is worthy and that which accrues benefit beyond the interests of self.

---

[1] Denton, Michael, Nature's Destiny: How the Laws of Biology Reveal Purpose in the Universe (New York: Free Press, 1998), p. 389.
[2] Used with permission
[3] Ferguson, Marilyn, The Aquarian Conspiracy (New York: G.P. Putman Sons, 1980), p. 417, (paraphrase).

ABOUT THE EDITORS

Grace K.F. Bates holds a Master of Science degree from the University of Hawaii. She first became acquainted with the founder of the profession, M. Lucille Kinlein in 1978 while a graduate student. That same year, she began studying with the Founder and was certified as a Pioneer in the Practice of Kinlein in 1983. Mrs. Bates entered the profession with a rich background in practice, teaching and writing in another field. She had held faculty appointments at the University of Hawaii (Kapiolani Community College) and the University of New Mexico. She was a published author of several textbooks. After certification, Mrs. Bates opened the first practice of Kinlein in Hawaii. Currently, she holds a faculty appointment at the Institute of Kinlein, Hyattsville, Maryland. She has written several articles about the profession. She lives and practices in Old Saybrook, Connecticut. Mrs. Bates is married and has one adult son.

Mary Louise Fenske Bolin put down her first roots in the rich farmland of Northwestern Montana then stretched out her branches in the breathtaking landscape of Alaska. She received a Master of Science Degree in Nursing from Montana State University in 1969 and promptly moved north. After a number of years teaching Community Health Aides in bush Alaska, she accepted a position with the University of Alaska, Anchorage, as Associate Professor. Mrs. Bolin began her study with M. Lucille Kinlein in 1979. She is certified as a Pioneer in the practice of kinlein through the Institute of Kinlein in Hyattsville, Maryland. Mrs. Bolin has been in private practice as a kinleiner for over 30 years. As an extension of her practice she has taught classes for the public on a variety of topics including communication, organizational integrity, and family relationships using the kinlein theory as a framework. She is at present on the faculty of the Institute of Kinlein and has written and published internally a number of articles pertaining to the profession.

About the Editors

Loretta Ulmschneider, C.P.K. has had a lifelong interest in learning about ways to help people build on something that is already inside of them. She has a B.A. degree and was certified as a Montessori teacher. Her study of the theories developed by Lucille Kinlein began in 1981 and she was certified in the practice of kinlein in 1984. She has studied Kinlein's theory of teaching since 1993, and taught courses for beginning students. She is a faculty member of the Institute of Kinlein.

INDEX